HUMAN SETTLEMENTS:
The Environmental Challenge

A Compendium of United Nations Papers
Prepared for the Stockholm Conference
on the Human Environment 1972

CENTRE FOR HOUSING,
BUILDING AND PLANNING
UNITED NATIONS DEPARTMENT OF
ECONOMIC AND SOCIAL AFFAIRS

Macmillan

First published 1974 by
THE MACMILLAN PRESS LTD
London and Basingstoke
Associated companies in New York
Dublin Melbourne Johannesburg and Madras

SBN 333 14071 0

Typeset in Great Britain by
PREFACE LIMITED
Salisbury, Wilts, England
and printed in Great Britain by
LEWIS REPRINTS LTD
Member of the Brown, Knight and Truscott Group
London and Tonbridge

The twin challenges posed by development and environment also offer us a double opportunity: to shape man's economic and social activities so that they harmonise as never before with the constraints imposed by nature; and to make nature serve the needs of all men.

U THANT

Contents

Foreword

Man's intervention in nature has engendered conflict between the natural and man-made environments. Only in this century has the resulting damage exceeded nature's capacity to redress the balance. Unprecedented population growth, industrialisation pursued almost as an end in itself and unregulated urbanisation have brought the man-made and natural environments into conflict to such a degree that not only is sound economic and social development endangered, but also the physical, social, aesthetic and spiritual well-being of man is jeopardised. Again and again we are reminded that controls are slipping out of his hands and that man's creations might ultimately consume him.

Fortunately, mankind is awakening to these challenges, as is evident in part from the United Nations Conference on the Human Environment in Stockholm, Sweden, in 1972. It brought together leading scientists and statesmen, defined the basic issues and recommended a course of action for the developing as well as the industrialised countries. The Conference rightly noted that development and environmental protection are not mutually opposed and that the developing countries, while sharing the experience of the industrialised societies, would do well to avoid environmental errors.

I am happy to note that this book describes the essential problems and possible solutions concerning human settlements as conceived by the professional community and considered by representatives of Governments at the Stockholm Conference, as well as by the United Nations General Assembly at its twenty-seventh session in 1972.

This volume, I trust, will advise and inspire experts, administrators and community leaders alike in discharging their unavoidable responsibility to redirect the forces that shape human settlements, to bring the man-made elements of the environment into closer harmony with the natural elements, to prevent further environmental impairment and to improve the quality of human life.

Technology as well as political and social organisation may be profoundly affected in meeting fully the demands for environmentally safe urban and rural settlements with decent shelter and community facilities. It is easy to see why if one ponders the implications of just two tasks which face mankind. First, it is necessary to build every year on the average until the end of this century the equivalent of sixty-seven new cities of one million inhabitants each in order to accommodate the increased urban population of the world. Second, over 1000 million new dwellings must be constructed by the end of this century to house the peoples of the world.

We must not demur in evolving new solutions; otherwise, in the words of Francis Bacon, 'He that will not apply new remedies must expect new evils'.

PHILIPPE DE SEYNES
Under-Secretary-General for Economic and Social Affairs

Preface

This book is a by-product of the prodigious efforts that scholars and leaders of the world made in understanding and meeting the greatest challenge of our time, namely the deterioration of the human environment, including human settlements. In the process of preparing background papers for the consideration of the United Nations Conference on the Human Environment, not only was a large mass of up-to-date information gathered, but certain ideas were crystallised which constitute a useful and instructive study in their own right.

In 1968, the General Assembly of the United Nations made the historic decision to convene the first United Nations Conference on the Human Environment, which was held at Stockholm, Sweden, in 1972. The General Assembly entrusted the organisation of the Conference to the Secretary-General of the United Nations and established a Preparatory Committee composed of representatives of twenty-seven Member States to advise him. The Secretary-General of the United Nations established a secretariat for the Environment Conference to direct and coordinate Conference preparations under the leadership of Mr Maurice Strong as Secretary-General of the Conference.

The Preparatory Committee selected six main themes for deliberation at the Conference; 'The Planning and Management of Human Settlements for Environment Quality' was one of these. The Committee also specified the subject areas to be considered under each theme. For the theme concerning human settlements, fifteen subject areas were chosen, each of which was the topic of a background report. On the basis of these reports the Conference Secretariat drew up the official Conference document on this theme.

The Centre for Housing, Building and Planning, a unit of the Department of Economic and Social Affairs of the Secretariat, is a focal point of the United Nations system in this field. The Centre's activities are directly or indirectly related to the development, protection and improvement of the human settlements environment. It was therefore asked to prepare most of the reports and co-ordinate others for the theme 'The Planning and Management of Human Settlements for Environment Quality', which falls within the competence of several units of the United Nations Secretariat and its specialised agencies. The subject areas chosen were the following:

Comprehensive Development Planning
Management of Settlements Development
Population Growth and Distribution
Rural Development
Housing and Related Facilities
Transitional and Marginal Areas
Recreation and Leisure
Interaction between Building and the
    Environment of Human Settlements
The Problems of Central City Areas
The Environment of the Central Areas
    of Cities: A Case Study of Warsaw
Industry
Transport and Communication
Water Supply, Sewage and Waste Disposal
Human Health and Welfare Factors
Social, Cultural and Aesthetic Factors

Though of high professional quality, the papers on the above subjects were not intended to be original. They rather reviewed and analysed current problems in each subject area, indicated matters of highest priority needing immediate attention and proposed certain action.

Since this valuable material is not available for general distribution, I am pleased that Macmillan has undertaken to publish it in an integrated form, together with the related decisions of the Conference and the General Assembly.

This book represents the contributions and efforts of a large number of individuals from the United Nations and its specialised agencies, as well as specialists and consultants from many parts of the world. We wish to express our deepest appreciation to all of them.

It must be emphasised that the views expressed herein are not necessarily those of the United Nations Conference on the Human Environment or of the Conference Secretariat. The Centre alone is responsible for them.

R. J. CROOKS
Director, Centre for Housing, Building and Planning

Acknowledgement

The Centre for Housing, Building and Planning of the United Nations expresses its deep appreciation to Mr John Ardill and Mr Derek Senior for their combined efforts in assembling into an integrated structure the fifteen papers on diverse subjects related to human settlements which constitute the basis of this volume. Indeed, their achievement goes far beyond editing, in many cases, to substantive writing in linking these papers to the central theme of the book.

Part One

1 The Problem

Man and his Environment

The relationship between man and his environment is mutual, complex and subtle. Each shapes and is shaped by the other. Man depends for his ultimate survival on the quality and quantity of the elements which make up his environment, but in the course of drawing upon them for his support he changes them and the natural relationship between them. When he farms he uses up nutrients in the soil; when he mines and manufactures he removes irreplaceable resources from the ground and changes them; when he consumes he leaves behind wastes which pollute and damage the environment. Above all when he joins with others to form settlements he puts in motion an intricate dynamic system of interrelationships between himself and his environment which profoundly influences his own present well-being and that of future generations.

The detrimental effects on the environment of man's activities now extend even to the most remote and inaccessible parts of the globe, where man himself seldom if ever ventures. The depths of the oceans and the ice of the polar regions are tainted by the wastes he so carelessly throws to the winds and the waters. But it is in his settlements, those parts of the global environment where the majority of men spend the greater part of their lives, where their social and economic activities are most densely concentrated, and where the opportunities for individual and collective satisfaction and advancement are greatest, that the most dramatic changes take place and the most intense conflicts occur. It follows that it is here too that the quality of the environment is particularly critical to man's health, welfare and happiness.

The need to give priority to the environment of settlements is underlined by the current trends in population growth, which suggest that by the end of the century the population of the world may be approximately double what it is today, and that the proportion living in towns and cities

3

may have increased from 40 per cent to 50 per cent of the total. In the developing world, where the greater part of this increase is expected to occur, current trends suggest that the urban population may jump from 25 per cent to 43 per cent of the total — in absolute numbers an increase from 600 million to 2100 million. These figures represent only the population of towns of more than 20,000 people so that the number living in settlements of all kinds is likely to be very much larger. But if the largest growth is to take place in the already overcrowded and environmentally degraded cities of the developing world it is hard to see how they can cope even minimally with such a tidal wave of people unless they adopt a radically different approach to urbanisation and the environment.

The main purpose of this book is to demonstrate that in the formulation of international, national, regional and local policies for the optimum use of the planet which is our home planning and management of the human settlements should be recognised as the chief means of assuring an appropriate environment for human survival and development.

This raises the fundamental question of how environmental considerations can be reconciled with the development of settlements. It is a crucial issue because the conventional approaches to 'the environment' and to urban development are essentially different. Concern for the environment tends to manifest itself in programmes to protect, preserve or restore the *status quo*. Plans and policies for urban development, on the other hand, are mainly directed towards changing the *status quo*.

It is clearly impossible to maintain the existing environment of our settlements while simultaneously seeking to further their economic and social development. Rather we must seek to create an urban environment which both facilitates economic and social development and enhances human health, welfare and happiness. This in turn means that policies and programmes concerned with promoting economic and social development must take into account the environmental consequences of the activities involved. The answer therefore lies in the adoption of a comprehensive approach to the planning and management of human

settlements. Traditional approaches along narrow sectoral
lines generally ignore the consequences of one set of activities
upon other activities and interests, particularly where such
consequences are not directly reflected in measurable costs.
Comprehensive planning provides a means of minimising
conflicts and undesirable side-effects by co-ordinating policy
objectives and sectoral plans and programmes.

A Question of Perspective

Before proceeding with an analysis of the environmental and
planning problems of settlements it is essential to examine
the differences in the way these problems are perceived in the
developed and the developing worlds and to consider some of
the unique environmental features of settlements in developing countries where the greatest challenge is coupled with the
greatest opportunity.

It is often said that improvement of the environment is
really the special problem of developed nations. The developing world, it is argued, lacking resources and facing the urgent
need to industrialise and to provide minimal public services,
cannot afford the luxury of additional investment to enhance
the environment. Developing countries, the argument goes,
would like nothing better than to find themselves in the
situation of the developed nations. They want heavy industry, large urban centres, higher national and per capita
incomes and so on. If these aims entail air and water
pollution, traffic congestion, noise, mental stress and all the
other problems and maladies that are endemic to the
urbanised areas of the world, well, such are the costs of being
rich and one has to be rich before one can start to channel
part of the national income towards the solution of environmental problems.

Implicit in this argument, of course, is the seemingly
plausible assumption that environmental problems are the
unavoidable by-product of development. This could not be
further from the truth; for it takes into account neither the
historical evolution of urban growth in the developed world
nor the opportunities that are open to developing countries
to tread a different path in the light of the experience of

those who have gone before them and in response to their own peculiar situation.

Generally speaking, the developed regions of the world passed through the first stages of industrialisation and urbanisation in an unplanned and disjointed fashion. These nations have indeed achieved high levels of national and personal prosperity, but the process has produced a large number of unanticipated ill-effects which today threaten both the quality of the environment and the achievement of further growth. The environmental problems facing those countries include unhealthy cities, dysfunctional physical layout of infrastructure and land uses, growing social problems and discontents and, in some areas, acute biological hazards. It is clear that correcting the mistakes of the past will be extremely costly and will involve radical changes in cultural values and attitudes, in legislation and in the physical structure of cities and towns.

But for developing nations standing at the threshold of industrialisation the crucial question is not 'How can the consequences of past errors be rectified?' but 'Must the mistakes of others be repeated?' The contention of this book is that such mistakes need not and must not be repeated. The developing nations are handicapped by a number of serious constraints, including a lack of financial resources, inadequate administrative machinery, a shortage of trained manpower and the need to achieve immediate economic benefits; but these are no justification for attempting to follow the same path to prosperity as the now-developed nations. The lesson of the past is that unco-ordinated and spontaneous development does not cost less than planned development. The developing nations are now at a point where individual cities and the national and regional networks of cities can be planned in such a way that many of the qualities of the natural environment which the developed nations are forced to restore at enormous cost can be protected and enhanced from the outset.

In the developed world the adoption of a more comprehensive system for the planning and guidance of the development process will inevitably lead to expensive redevelopment and renewal schemes. The developing countries, on the other hand, free as they are to make use of the same knowledge and understanding of the development process and the latest techniques of environmental planning and management, have the opportunity to build new types of settlement in which the natural and man-made components are in greater harmony, and to do so at no significantly greater cost than would be incurred in allowing unplanned development to take place.

Special Problems of Developing Countries

In the developing world comprehensive planning is being introduced into cultural and institutional frameworks which differ greatly from those of the developed world; it is also being called upon to solve some historically unique problems. In order to judge what contribution it can make, therefore, it is necessary to examine some of the distinguishing features of urbanisation in the developing countries.

Firstly, the rate of population increase in the developing world — resulting largely from major improvements in health — and the sheer scale of urbanisation in these countries are unprecedented in the history of man. The expansion of urban structures and services to meet this growth, and the demands the urban population will make upon rural areas for food, resources. and recreational opportunities, pose monumental problems. At the same time these countries have rapidly growing rural populations. Comprehensive development policies must, therefore, take into account both urban and rural environments if irreversible environmental damage is to be avoided. Probably nothing is more urgently needed in developing countries than ways of guiding both urban growth and rural development processes so that social and economic objectives are balanced with environmental considerations.

Secondly, unlike urban growth in most of the developed countries, the growth of large cities in the developing countries is preceding the economic growth necessary to sustain large urban agglomerations. There is a headlong rush to the big cities even in countries where natural resources are underdeveloped and the tools of production and capital investment are woefully inadequate. In Europe and North America migration to the towns, though it involved many problems and hardships for the new migrants, roughly matched the course of urban industrialisation and economic growth. Industries sprang up where the natural conditions favoured their establishment and cities grew around the industry. In the developing world the rapidly growing cities are mostly residential, and many of the residential areas are not of a very permanent nature. The urban structure of most of these cities has not yet solidified. Thus, when the necessary industries are introduced, their location can be planned in the light of environmental considerations so as to achieve a rational physical relationship between industrial, commercial, residential and other land-using activities and an optimal system of transport networks to tie them together.

Thirdly, agriculture in developing countries has not produced the food surplus which predated the growth of cities in Europe and North America. Rural areas neither produce enough food for the cities nor provide an adequate market for goods manufactured in the cities. Thus rural poverty and urban poverty reinforce each other. This poses a dilemma: should priority be given to tackling poverty and unemployment in the cities or in the rural areas? Arguments can be advanced for either course, but is the poor themselves who will probably decide the issue, for most of them believe they are or will be better off in the cities. There is a certain credibility in this view because improvements are often easier to organise in the cities than in rural areas with dispersed populations. But even if the current problems of urban poverty and unemployment can be dealt with, the fundamental imbalance between population and food supplies in developing countries remains. Recent advances in agricultural technology are increasing productivity but can only relieve the food shortage for about two decades – a short period within which to attempt to achieve a better balance between population and resources. And meanwhile they are displacing labour and speeding the flow of unskilled workers to the cities.

Fourthly, since urbanisation is increasing at a faster pace than industrialisation, the cities of the developing world are evolving a largely service economy which lacks the support of manufacturing industry. The developed nations progressed from an agricultural economy to an industrial economy and then to a service economy. The developing countries have jumped directly to a service economy. Their urban areas are cities in the demographic sense but not in terms of the activities which they house. A large proportion of the population consists of 'odd-job men who live on the rim of starvation'. Unemployment, underemployment and poverty are commonplace and lead to apathy, idleness and despair. This in turn destroys initiative and concern for both the immediate home environment and the larger urban environment. Nevertheless this vast army of the unemployed and underemployed is a human resource which could be mobilised for environmental improvement.

It should be evident from this brief outline of the differences in urban growth between the developed and the developing nations that there is no logic in attempts by the latter to copy the past example of the former. Indeed one might guess that to do so in the unique situation of the developing countries would very likely create new, additional and unpredictable problems. There are, of course, similarities in all settlements, in both the developed and the developing world. Initially, the common denominators of the urban condition enable us to examine the general concept of the environment of human settlements. But this general analysis must be refined by an examination of the differences in the processes of urbanisation and the basic issues involved in developing a healthy environment in various social and economic situations.

The Human Settlement

The human settlement is a complex organism composed of many man-made elements performing complex functions and set within the natural environment. Man-made and natural elements together comprise the territorial habitat within which man lives, works, raises his family and seeks his physical, spiritual and intellectual well-being. Many of urban man's needs are met from beyond the boundaries of his settlement, and much of rural man's working day may be spent beyond its confines, but the quality of both the natural and man-made elements in its environment are crucial to all aspects of human life and to the ability of the settlement itself to function effectively.

Many human activities alter the topography, vegetation and animal life of the area in which they take place, thus disturbing the natural equilibrium and modifying the natural environment. These environmental changes often result in deleterious effects on the physical and mental well-being of man himself. Obviously, not all man's interferences with the natural order are of this character. Many have proved beneficial both to man and to the total environment: the draining of swamps and the elimination of mosquitoes, for example, have produced entirely salutary results. But in the places where man's activities are most densely concentrated — his settlements — the environmental impact is greatest and the risks of environmental damage are most acute.

When he builds a settlement man introduces into the natural environment a great variety of structures and activities: houses, factories, commercial districts, social services and facilities, parks and playing fields, water-supply and sewerage systems, transport and communication networks, electricity and gas grids. There is a constant process of interaction within and between these groups of structures and infrastructures and between them and the natural elements. The mere existence of man-made elements creates conflicts with the natural environment: it alters the course of streams and the run-off of rain-water; it modifies the speed and direction of airflows; it changes the way in which the sun's heat is absorbed and reflected. But the conflicts become more complex and dramatic when human activities are performed within this physical framework. Only then are the problems of air and water pollution, noise, traffic congestion and waste disposal created. These activities and their consequences not only interfere with the natural environment; they also by their juxtaposition with other human activities give rise to secondary conflicts which impair the operation of many activities.

Thus the environmental quality of a residential area, which depends primarily on the quality of its houses, infrastructure and facilities and their spatial arrangement, can be grossly impaired by the existence of a nearby industrial area, an airport or a major highway; or conversely, by lack of access to other parts of the city where the residents must work, shop and seek much of their recreation and social life. Similarly the environmental quality of a city centre depends not only on the quality and layout of the buildings but also on the extent to which the activities carried out there, and particularly the various flows of goods and people through and within the centre, conflict with one another, and the way in which the central district is physically related to other quarters of the city.

Resolving the Conflicts

The conflicts springing from the physical interrelationships and juxtaposition of various urban functions can be resolved — or at least minimised — by comprehensive planning and development control. That is to say, given an understanding of how urban systems function and interrelate, a clear picture of the number and kind of activities and people to be catered for, and a predetermined set of integrated objectives, the location and form of industries, commercial districts, residential areas and other urban functions can be consciously designed so that mutually incompatible activities are physically separated yet efficiently linked by transport networks. A deliberate arrangement of urban functions, aimed at enhancing the quality of the environment, can have other benefits too. The concentration of industry in carefully selected locations, for instance, enables firms to share technical and infrastructural facilities and allows those facilities to be provided at lower unit costs than would otherwise be possible.

In established, highly developed yet unplanned cities, the rearrangement of existing functions to bring them into harmony with one another and with the natural environment is clearly an expensive proposition. In new towns, however, and often in the cities of the developing world, where many of the existing structures are impermanent, industrial activity is minimal and highways and other infrastructures have not been developed to the point where they predetermine the location of other structures and activities, comprehensively integrated development is much easier and less costly.

Individual towns and cities cannot, however, be planned in isolation, for all settlements are linked together in a complex dynamic system and each interacts with the non-settled environment. Urban planning must, therefore, be carried out within the framework of comprehensive national and regional plans and policies, and machinery must be established at both national and regional level to ensure that the guidelines thus laid down are duly observed.

2 Evolution of Human Settlements

Population Growth and Urbanisation

The population of the world is growing at an unprecedented rate. Many believe and fear that the day is not far distant when it will outstrip the earth's capacity to provide for man's essential needs, particularly at the high levels of material comfort and sophistication to which a large part of the population is already accustomed and an even larger part is aspiring. But whatever steps may be taken to curb the rate of growth, they cannot affect the situation in which many now find themselves and which many more will experience by the end of this century. For it is not only the total population that is growing fast: so too is the rate at which men are coming together in large settlements, and it is in these concentrations of human life and activity that the relationship between man and his environment is most complex, most difficult to plan and manage and most crucial to man's happiness, prosperity and welfare.

Malthus, who was the first political economist to consider seriously the relationship between man and his environment, was concerned with only one aspect of the environment — its ability to supply food — and he implicitly assumed a constant technology. The conditions of malnutrition and mortality he observed in Europe were rather similar to those prevailing today in backward areas, particularly in remote areas where technologies are primitive. Where technologies have been improved and the problem of food supply is at least temporarily under control, we are beginning to realise that the earth's capacity to produce food is not the only environmental constraint upon the human population. There are limits to the supply of non-renewable resources; there are limits to the amount of air and water pollution that can be tolerated; there are limits of sheer space, for even where people are concentrated in large numbers on relatively small areas of land they make large and growing demands upon the whole land mass for food, water and raw materials, and as an occasional refuge from urban life.

Accelerated growth and increasing urbanisation, which are the outstanding features of world population trends in the modern age, are comparatively recent phenomena. For most of man's time on earth the total population probably never approached 500 million. But from the seventeenth century, when it did reach 500 million, it has been growing rapidly and at an increasing rate. Soon after 1800 the world had acquired another 500 million. Another 500 million was added by 1880, a fourth by 1925, a fifth by 1950, a sixth by 1960 and a seventh by 1968, with the result that the world now contains more than 3500 million people. Within another fifteen years, it is estimated, there will be 1000 million more people and by the year 2000 the world may contain well over 6000 million — almost double the present figure. The question we must face, therefore, is how can we at least double our organisational and technological capacity to live on earth without making it incapable of supporting further life.

All available evidence and all predictions based on present knowledge make it clear that to rescue the human environ-

Table 1   Population of the world, more developed and less developed regions, and major world areas, 1950-2000 (in millions)

Area	1950	1960	1970	1980	1990	2000	2000 per 100 in 1970
World total	2486	2982	3635	4467	5456	6515	179
More dev. regions	858	976	1091	1210	1337	1454	133
Less dev. regions	1628	2005	2545	3257	4120	5061	199
Europe	392	425	462	497	533	568	123
Soviet Union	180	214	243	271	302	330	136
Northern America	166	199	228	261	299	333	146
Oceania	13	16	19	24	30	35	184
South Asia	698	865	1126	1486	1912	2354	209
East Asia	657	780	930	1095	1265	1424	153
Africa	217	270	344	457	616	818	238
Latin America	162	213	283	377	500	652	230

Figure 1 Estimated and conjectured size of the world's population, 1750-2000, more developed and less developed regions

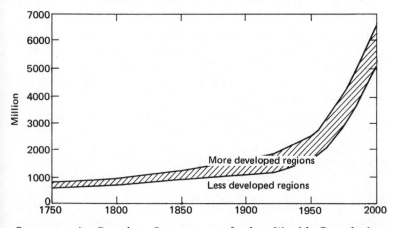

Source: *A Concise Summary of the World Population Situation in 1970* (New York: United Nations, 1971. Sales No.: E.71.XIII.2).

ment we must in the long run slow down the rate of population growth and ultimately bring it into harmony with the availability of natural resources. But in the meantime large increases in population remain inevitable. Moreover, we must remember that most of the adult population which will be alive in the year 2000 — above all, most of those who between now and the end of the century will reach an age when they increase the demand for houses and jobs and all the services and facilities which support houses and jobs — have already been born.

Until quite recently man's habitat was largely rural. Although some ancient cities are remembered for their decisive contributions to civilisation, even the largest of them were small by modern standards. They were also few in number and cannot have contained any appreciable proportion of the world's population. It is thought that in 1800 only three per cent of the world's population lived in towns of 5000 or more, and by modern standards the environment

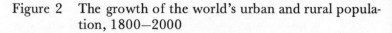

Figure 2   The growth of the world's urban and rural population, 1800—2000

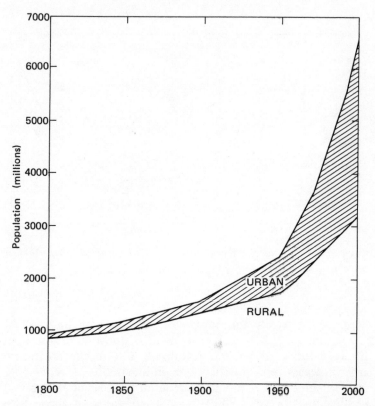

Sources: Data for 1800, 1950, 1900 adapted from estimates made by Kingsley Davis and Hilda Harts as published in P. M. Hauser (editor), *Urbanisation in Asia and the Far East* (Calcutta: UNESCO, 1957) p. 56. In these estimates urban population is defined as population in localities with 5000 or more inhabitants. Data for 1950 through 2000 are from 'Urban and Rural Population: Individual Countries 1950–1965, and Regions and Major Areas, 1950–2000' (United Nations Population Division Working Paper ESA/P/WP.33/Rev.1, 22 September 1970). In these estimates the official urban definitions observed in each individual country were used.

of most small towns of that period was probably more rural than urban. Even today in some of the less developed countries small towns have few urban features: in India, for example, many settlements with 5000 inhabitants are virtually villages.

It is estimated that in 1800 the total urban population of the world was 27 million. Today the world's two largest agglomerations (centred on Tokyo and New York) alone contain more than 27 million inhabitants, while the total urban population has increased fifty-fold. The rural population meanwhile has grown to nearly 2500 million. By the year 2000 the urban and rural populations may be in balance at about 3200 million each.

The percentage of the population living in urban areas has been rising rapidly. Beginning at about three per cent in 1800 it had reached more than 6 per cent in 1850 and almost 14 per cent in 1900: today it is approaching 40 per cent. There is a wide difference, however, between the more and the less developed parts of the world. In the developed regions over half the population was already urban by 1950. The figure is now more than 65 per cent and by the year 2000 it may be about 80 per cent. The truly rural man will therefore be statistically rare in these regions. In the developing world

Table 2   Urban population of the world, more developed and less developed regions, and major world areas, 1950-2000 (in millions)

Area	1950	1960	1970	1980	1990	2000	2000 per 100 in 1970
World total	704	935	1352	1854	2517	3329	246
More dev. regions	439	582	717	864	1021	1174	164
Less dev. regions	265	403	635	990	1496	2155	339
Europe	207	246	292	339	388	438	150
Soviet Union	71	106	139	174	214	252	181
Northern America	106	138	169	204	245	284	168
Oceania	8	10	13	17	21	25	192
South Asia	111	154	238	370	556	793	333
East Asia	105	179	266	387	541	722	271
Africa	30	48	77	125	203	320	416
Latin America	66	103	158	238	350	495	313

only about 25 per cent of the population is urban now but the figure is expected to grow to about 40 per cent by the year 2000.

In absolute numbers, however, the picture is different. In 1970 the developed countries still had more town dwellers than the developing countries, but during the 1970s the urban population of the developing world will probably overtake that of the developed world, and by the end of the century it will be considerably greater. At the same time the rural population of developing countries (which has been

Figure 3   Urban and rural population, in more developed and less developed regions, 1950-2000

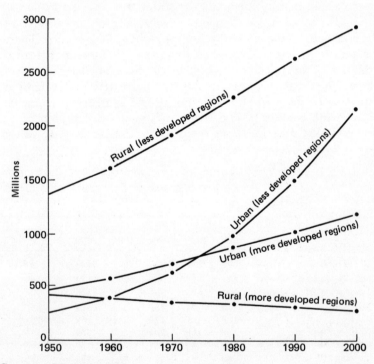

Source: United Nations: *A Concise Summary of the World Population Situation in 1970,* Population Studies, No. 48 (New York: United Nations, 1971).

Table 3   Urban and rural population and percentage of urban population in more developed and less developed regions, 1950-2000

Year	More developed regions Population (millions)		Per-centage Urban	Less developed regions Population (millions)		Per-centage Urban
	Urban	Rural		Urban	Rural	
1950	439	418	51	265	1363	16
1960	582	394	60	403	1603	20
1970	717	374	66	635	1910	25
1980	864	347	71	990	2267	30
1990	1021	316	76	1496	2623	36
2000	1174	280	81	2155	2906	43

rising since the mid century) will continue to rise, while the rural population of developed countries (which has been falling since mid century) will continue to fall. Whereas the rural population of developing regions was about three times that of developed regions at mid century, it will be about ten times as large by the year 2000.

While the percentage of people in urban areas has been growing the size of large settlements has also been increasing enormously, their nature has been changing, and to some extent the difference between urban and rural areas has been growing less distinct. For centuries most towns were for the most part widely separated small enclaves, usually fortified. In form and in their economic and social role they contrasted sharply with the surrounding countryside: there was no problem of distinguishing between urban and rural areas. With the industrial revolution, when large factories replaced home and shop crafts, cities began to grow in size and became even more distinct, with their tall chimneys and railway yards. Their outer edges, however, began to blur as they extended into the countryside.

About a century ago a new urban form started to appear in western Europe as previously separate cities began to coalesce. With the emergence of these conurbations it became difficult to distinguish between, on the one hand, a single city and, on the other hand, a group of cities which retained their own central areas, local institutions and municipal authorities yet increasingly functioned as one entity. A similar pattern has since developed in most parts of the world. In advanced countries it has been supplemented by the growth of 'out-of-town' industrial estates and shopping centres, which introduce urban features into the countryside without giving rise to distinctive towns.

Even so it was still possible towards the end of the nineteenth century to define a 'great city' as one having 100,000 or more inhabitants.[1] Today a city of that size can no longer be considered great except in the most sparsely populated parts of the globe. In 1970 there were 174 cities of more than one million inhabitants, 50 of them with at least 2.5 million.[2] But large cities were still rare in the developing world as recently as 1920; at that date, says a United Nations report,[3] only 20 per cent of the urban population in the developing regions lived in cities of 500,000 or more inhabitants: in developed regions the corresponding figure was already 47 per cent. By 1960, however, these figures had grown to 43 per cent in the developing world and 49 per cent in the developed world, so that there was no longer a marked difference in this respect.

Drastic alterations in settlement patterns can result from the unequal rate of growth of big cities and smaller towns — notably changes in the extent to which urban centres are concentrated or dispersed within a region and changes in the form of the rural habitat. Under changing conditions, conventional descriptions become inadequate. Settlements which seem 'urban' from one point of view may still appear 'rural' from another. Certainly the redefinition of rural areas as urban for administrative purposes generally lags far behind the fact of urbanisation. The present fluidity of the concepts of 'urban' and 'rural' is itself an indication of the change in the nature of settlements which has come about with the changes in population distribution. With the increase in the number of urban attributes and their wider distribution it is doubtful whether the historical distinction between urban and rural areas will retain its relevance much longer. Neither administrative status nor type of economic activity can be relied upon as a permanent criterion. The one distinguishing feature of strictly urban areas which is likely to keep its significance for practical purposes is the concentration of numerous residents within relatively compact areas of dense settlement.

Further increases in the number of large cities must be expected, but it is less certain that we shall see a continuing increase in the number of people living within the boundaries of a single built-up area — the form which historically defines the city. Increasingly, the tendency is for large cities to be surrounded by a number of smaller towns which serve specialised functions as industrial or residential areas. According to such writers as Jane Jacobs[4] and Hoover and Vernon[5], smaller towns tend to attract old-established industrial firms which no longer depend on the specialised external economies available in large cities and have increased their scale of production to a point where they need cheaper sites for large factories. The spaces between some major conurbations are already becoming filled in with satellite towns and residential areas separated by relatively narrow stretches of country. This is the settlement pattern we call megalopolis.

The concept of megalopolis is still vague: no example has yet been defined as an administrative unit with precise boundaries. Statisticians attempting to estimate the populations of megalopolitan areas have adopted various criteria, usually based on population density. The three regions presently recognised as megalopolitan may each be approaching a population of 50 million. The Tokaido megalopolis, a coalescence of Japan's three largest metropolitan areas (Tokyo, Osaka and Nagoya), contains about half the country's total population. The Atlantic seaboard megalopolis of the United States stretches from Boston in the north through New York, Philadelphia and Baltimore to Washington. The third such area extends over several countries of northern Europe including all of Belgium, most of the Netherlands, a large part of Western Germany, the northern rim of France and the south-east of England.

Thus in less than a century we have come from a world in which cities of 100,000 people could be regarded as exceptional to one in which urban systems of 50 million inhabitants are evident.

The largest urban settlements today serve unique functions in the organisation of international trade and in industrial innovation and management. The rapid emergence of such massive units of settlement has, however, brought with it acute planning problems. The essential need is to anticipate the long-term effects at the outset, so that efficient solutions can be formulated to the problems caused by megalopolitan growth before they become critical. But the finest statistical analysis will be of no use without government machinery to implement the indicated policies. Unfortunately megalopolis no respecter of administrative boundaries and its gigantic extent greatly exceeds any existing regional unit of government.

The Pattern of Rural Settlement

Varied sizes and densities of settlement can be found in rural areas too. This has important implications for planning: the way the rural population is dispersed through the countryside can be crucial to the success of rural development policies. Road networks are likely to remain sparse where there are many small settlements widely scattered, for roads can only be maintained economically when they connect substantial villages or towns. Schools, hospitals, co-operatives, electricity

Table 4   Rural population of the world, more developed and less developed regions, and major world areas, 1950-2000 (in millions)

Area	1950	1960	1970	1980	1990	2000	2000 per 100 in 1970
World total	1782	1997	2283	2614	2939	3186	140
More dev. regions	418	394	374	347	316	280	75
Less dev. regions	1363	1603	1910	2267	2623	2906	152
Europe	185	179	170	158	145	131	77
Soviet Union	109	108	104	97	89	77	74
Northern America	60	60	59	56	54	50	85
Oceania	5	5	6	7	9	10	167
South Asia	587	711	888	1116	1355	1561	176
East Asia	552	601	664	708	725	703	106
Africa	187	221	268	332	413	498	186
Latin America	97	110	125	139	150	157	126

and other factors of development are also easier to provide where the population is relatively concentrated. It is particularly important that there should be a good scatter of small market towns to bring services and professional help and advice within the reach of villagers and peasants. But villages which depend on farming can grow too large for their accessible farmland.

In some industrialised countries the difference in standard of living between urban and rural areas is disappearing, but in developing countries the distinction between the two remains clearly marked, with important consequences for planners and administrators. There are, however, problems of definition. While it is generally accepted that a rural area is one in which agriculture, forestry or fishing predominates and in which population densities are low, there is no consensus on what constitutes a rural settlement. Population criteria vary between as low as two hundred and as high as five thousand or more. Moreover, in many countries the rural population is enumerated without any break-down by type or size of settlement: it is simply what is left when the urban population is subtracted from the total. There are nevertheless several criteria which may serve as a framework for discussing rural settlements in developing countries. In general there is a greater preponderance of 'natural' elements in the environment than in urban areas; the population is mainly engaged in agriculture, using land extensively and without the benefit of modern technologies; people are isolated, conservative in their attitudes and have fewer contacts with others; buildings are predominantly traditional in design, materials and construction and utilities and community services are scarce or lacking.

Rural settlement patterns may be characterised as 'dispersed' or 'clustered', but here again there is no general agreement as to how each category should be defined. The United Nations Seminar on Rural Housing and Community Facilities[6] considered the 'dispersed rural population' referred to families living in social and spatial isolation and defined the upper limit of a dispersed settlement as twenty people. By this criterion it was estimated that in Latin America about 35 per cent of the rural population lived in dispersed settlements. There are indications that in Africa the percentage may be much higher. But while 'dispersed' is generally associated with 'isolated' it has been observed in parts of Brazil, Colombia, Chile and other countries that dispersed settlements are linked by complex social and economic networks. The term 'dispersed' is also applied to the transitory settlements of nomadic people, which are found in many parts of the world, and not only in remote areas. In many countries temporary settlements for migratory workers are commonplace in agricultural areas at harvest time. Motorised nomadic groups gathering in camps form another variation. In the U.S.A., for example, mobile homes constitute 10 per cent of the housing stock.

'Clustered' settlements may be defined by the number of people or the distance between houses or by a combination of both factors. In form these larger settlements may be nucleated (arranged around some central feature such as a market place) or linear (strung out along a road or waterway). The physical structure of villages and the type of housing in them usually depends on cultural traits, the kind of agriculture practised, the climate and other factors. In India the village structure is often influenced by the caste system. In central and southern Africa it is influenced by the extended-family and tribal system. In Latin America the patterns introduced by Spanish colonists are still being followed wherever spontaneous settlement takes place, and are often adopted by professional planners.

Village houses in many tropical countries are flimsy and primitive. Often nothing more substantial is needed since most of the work and a great deal of family and social life takes place in the open. Where temperatures are comfortable, people often sleep outside on the ground or on rooftops. In colder climates — the High Andes of Peru and Bolivia for instance — the family may share their house with their livestock for warmth and safety.

In developing countries, generally speaking, there has been little change in the centuries-old tradition of village design and construction. Such improvement as has taken place has been mostly in the provision of public utilities. Even in western Europe, where settlement planning and rural housing standards have improved rapidly, there are still areas where housing and village facilities have advanced very little. In eastern Europe there have been great efforts to rationalise settlement patterns in order to increase agricultural production and facilitate the provision of community services.[7]

Generally the main problem is that rural planning and village design have been neglected fields. Rural settlements therefore tend to develop in an uncontrolled fashion, exposed to many environmental hazards, natural and man-made, and themselves sometimes cause environmental damage. Both of these tendencies could be avoided by proper planning. In particular the haphazard location of rural settlements lays them open to natural disasters and makes them liable to damage the natural environment. In many parts of the world rural settlements are located near rivers or creeks that periodically overflow and flood the surrounding areas. In tropical countries the retreating flood waters breed mosquitoes and other disease carriers. Where the best land is owned by wealthy farmers, as frequently occurs in the Andes, poorer peasants are forced to settle on steep slopes exposed to the danger of landslides. In other circumstances villages are located without regard to the risk of avalanches, hurricanes or tidal waves.

There always is some sort of rationale behind the location of settlements: commercial convenience, ease of access, security against attack or some other good reason. But no one reason, however valid, can ensure that the location is suitable for all aspects of human welfare. Comprehensive planning would take into account the whole range of factors essential to a rewarding and healthy environment.

In addition to the hazards of location most rural settlements in developing countries suffer environmental deficiencies of their own — notably poor housing, a lack of uncontaminated water and inadequate facilities for disposing of human, animal and household wastes. These problems are interrelated and often aggravated by acute poverty and rapid population growth. Absence of decent drinking water is perhaps the most common and crucial problem. Lacking centralised water-supply systems, most villages depend upon wells, tanks, ponds, rivers and lakes as sources of drinking water. In rural India about 99 per cent of households depend on a water source of doubtful wholesomeness which is usually more than one hundred yards from the house. Similar conditions prevail in several countries of Africa and Asia. Traditional building materials add to the health hazards by harbouring disease-bearing insects and rodents. In the Philippines, for instance, the typical rural dwelling has walls and roof of nipa or cogood grass and a slatted bamboo floor raised five feet or more above the ground on bamboo or wooden posts, the underfloor space being used to store agricultural products or to shelter animals. In Kenya most rural dwellings are built of mud and wattle with grass thatch. Generally, throughout the developing world, the use of organic building materials brings the dangers of fire, decomposition and weather damage.

In the rural regions of the tropics, in spite of a great deal of progress in public health, epidemic and endemic diseases remain a constant threat to millions of people. Although malaria has been eradicated in some areas, it remains man's most common disease, followed by snail fever (schistosomiasis). Intestinal infections are the most common cause of infant mortality. Onchocereiasis blinds enormous numbers of people. Yaws and guinea-worm strike down villagers at the beginning of the rainy season when they most need their health to plant their food crops.

In many rural areas man destroys the ability of the land to support him. Cutting down forests or burning scrub and grass-land for farming impoverishes the soil and may lead to the drying up of water courses and to soil erosion. More 'advanced' techniques can be equally damaging. Large irrigation reservoirs breed insects and change established life cycles, thereby threatening crops. Pesticides, while increasing agricultural output, may poison water courses. Large-scale mining, quarrying and logging and the introduction of mechanised industries have modified the environment by destroying natural features and generating pollutants. Some governments and entrepreneurs consider that environmental hazards are the price that has to be paid for industrialisation and development but many of these detrimental effects can be avoided by proper physical planning and regard for environmental consequences.

Migration and Urban Growth

The characteristic response in many parts of the world to the poverty, degrading environmental conditions and lack of opportunities for personal advancement in rural areas is migration to the towns. This happened during the industrial revolution in the now developed countries (where it still continues to a reduced extent) and it is happening today in many developing countries on a massive and frightening scale, bringing with it even greater environmental problems and dangers than those the migrant leaves behind him. For the migrant is not motivated solely, or even predominantly, by environmental considerations: the dominant factor has been and is chiefly economic.

The principal influences on population movements and on the location and growth of large settlements have been the industrial revolution, with its accompanying advances in transport and communications, and other aspects of modern technology and organisation. Underlying and reinforcing these technical trends are human and cultural factors — notably the principle of economic determinism, according to which those options which are seen to yield the greatest economic return are given priority. This principle, a legacy of man's long struggle against scarcity, has contributed to some of the most severe and unnecessary environmental ills of the twentieth century.

In the less industrialised parts of the world economic considerations are not the only factors. Others such as desire for better educational opportunities and access to public utilities and health and welfare services also play a role in stimulating migration. In these regions, in fact, urbanisation is now proceeding with greater momentum than industrialisation, with the result that the very amenities which attract the migrant become incapable of meeting the increased demands made upon them. The mass movement to the cities, together with the natural growth of urban population, has placed a severe strain on the fabric and facilities of many older cities and thus created some of the most squalid and degrading human environments.

The environmental side-effects of individuals' and society's desire for economic and social benefits are sometimes only a temporary phenomenon but in many rapidly growing cities, where the rate of in-migration exceeds for a sustained period the rate at which new jobs can be provided, diminishing returns occur.

The amount and rate of growth of the city are the crucial factors. Where the population growth is too massive and rapid to be absorbed by the existing city structures there may be irreparable damage to the physical, social, administrative and political elements necessary for satisfactory urban life. On the other hand, where the amount of growth is more moderate, or the rate is not too rapid, significant economic and social gains can be achieved without excessive environmental damage.

There has been much argument about whether rural-to-urban migration is stimulated mainly by the 'push' of adverse rural conditions or the 'pull' of urban attractions. Certainly particular negative factors can sometimes be attributed to rural areas, and positive ones to urban areas. On balance it is probably a matter of the town's comparative advantages. This may be particularly true of places where migration is followed by relatively permanent urban residence, as in Latin America. In much of Asia and Africa, however, a large proportion of migrants settle in towns only temporarily, eventually returning to their home areas. In India, where many married men are temporary migrants, their return home has been attributed to the 'push-back' factors in the cities, especially the insuperable housing shortage. In Africa many migrants are thought to have no intention of remaining in the cities any longer than it takes to accumulate some money. Since they remain countrymen at heart their return may be ascribed to a rural 'pull-back'.

The tendency of rural people to migrate to urban areas may be increased where relatives or neighbours have already gained a foothold in the city. From these the newcomers expect help and advice in finding a job and perhaps an offer of temporary accommodation, and they in turn will provide a similar service to another generation of migrants. Such 'chain-migration' can lead to the growth of ethnic and cultural ghettoes in the city, to the extent that adaptation to urban life may be impeded because the majority of social contacts take place within the group. The majority of migrants are young adults seeking their first job, with the result that the young adult work force is considerably strengthened in urban areas and weakened in rural areas. In most of Asia and Africa the majority of migrants are men; in Latin America there is a preponderance of women. There is a tendency for migrants to be better educated than the average person in rural areas, while falling short of urban standards. In addition migrants to big cities often include the most able and skilled among the inhabitants of small towns and regional centres — the businessmen and craftsmen and men and women trained in the professions.

But cities do not grow simply because of migration, nor does migration alone account for changes in the relative and absolute size of urban and rural populations. Changes in birth and death rates are equally significant. Discoveries in medicine, improved sanitation and education in public health concepts have brought the reduction, if not the eradication, of many fatal and debilitating diseases in most parts of the world. The consequent decline in death rates, or to put it another way, increase in life expectancy, leads to greater rates of natural increase unless it is matched by a comparable decline in birth rates.

In the developed countries these advances in medicine and public health came gradually during the second half of the nineteenth century and the early part of the twentieth century and were sometimes accompanied by decreases in birth rates — a trend reinforced recently by the widespread adoption of family planning. Hence the rate of natural population increase in these regions has been comparatively low, and in most of the richer countries is now only one per cent per annum or less. In the developing regions advances in medicine and public health have been recent, becoming significant from about 1945 onwards, and with the accumulated and more rapidly increasing body of knowledge the impact has been more sudden. Death rates have declined more steeply than they did in the comparable period in the developed countries; meanwhile, with a few exceptions — the Republic of Korea, the Ryukyu Islands and some parts of the Caribbean — the developing regions have experienced no marked decline in birth rates. (Improvements in general standards of health which are not accompanied by changes in cultural attitudes can lead to an increase birth rate.) Consequently population is now growing in the developing regions at rates which have no historical precedent.

These changes have different effects in urban and rural areas. In the past large cities were so unhealthy that they could be regarded as 'consumers' of population. If their population increased at all it was mostly due to migration. Now, with the concentration of public health and medical services in urban areas, most towns and cities have an appreciable rate of natural increase, often equal to that in rural areas. Where the natural increase rates are similar in both kinds of area the faster growth of urban populations stems mainly from migration (and, statistically, from the reclassification of previously rural areas). Often city populations grow at about twice the rate at which the national population is growing, suggesting a roughly equal contribution by natural increase and migration. Recent statistics from the Soviet Union show increases in urban population made up of 44 per cent from rural-to-urban migration, 41 per cent from natural increase and almost 15 per cent from reclassification. The proportions can vary widely, however. In the London region less than 30 per cent of the total increase between the early fifties and early sixties was due to migration, while in the same period in the Paris region the figure was about 60 per cent. In these cases much of the migration was probably inter-urban rather than rural-urban.

In developed countries, particularly those which already have a high proportion of town dwellers, internal migration can cause an absolute decline in the population of rural areas without significantly adding to the urban population. In such cases the migration pattern tends to be inter-urban, with moves from smaller to larger cities, and inter-rural, from remote settlements to ones nearer the cities. At the same time people are moving out from the centres of conurbations and metropolitan areas to suburbs and satellite towns, in some cases causing absolute population losses in central cities. The suburbs tend to have a higher proportion of young adults, giving them a higher rate of natural increase than the central cities.

In those parts of the developing world which have already reached a substantial level of urbanisation – many Latin American countries, for instance – natural increase may equal or exceed in-migration. In parts of Asia where cities have been long established but do not account for a high proportion of the total population, natural increase may also be the main element in urban growth, much of the in-migration being offset by return migration to rural areas. But where significant urban development is comparatively recent, as in many parts of Africa, migration is the dominant factor.

Since natural increase plays such an important part in urban population growth it is often thought that birth-control programmes can reduce the pressure on overstrained city structures. This may be true in the long run, but the greatest demand for jobs and houses comes from young adults, not babies, and as we have seen most migrants arrive in cities as young adults.

Transitional Settlements

Urbanisation is a complex, relentless process which occurs under the most diverse conditions throughout the world. We might suspect that its roots lie in something as basic as an instinctive human gregariousness. Whatever the cause, people increasingly seem to want to live in company with a large and varied collection of other people in a way which cannot happen in a rural environment.

The migratory stream which brings people together in large cities often occurs in successive stages. People from remote rural areas move to hamlets near a highway; those from hamlets move to small towns; small-town dwellers move to the central slums of the big city; those from the city centre move out to the periphery. For many, to migrate means to exchange one set of bad environmental conditions for another, probably worse, set.

The poor rural migrants arriving in the large towns and cities of the developing world today are being accommodated in two principal ways: either they descend on the old residential quarters of central cities, characterised by low incomes and low rentals, and there push up the occupation density and extend and intensify slum conditions; or else they invade vacant public or private land, usually on the city's edge, and build their own makeshift shelters from whatever materials come to hand. Sometimes the two forms overlap in that former migrants established as squatters provide rented accommodation to new migrants. In Latin America it has been found that the migrant seeks rented accommodation either in a city slum or in a squatter settlement while he seeks a job and adapts himself to urban life. The rent he has to pay commonly forms a very high percentage of his income and his employment is liable to be unstable, threatening his ability to pay rent at all. In these circumstances he is encouraged to seek a situation in which he is not at the mercy of a landlord and an employer. Thus, once he is established in the city – a process which may take several years – he will probably join an organised occupation of vacant land.

Squatter settlements formed in this way are by far the fastest-growing sector of urban areas in developing countries and they embody the most squalid, degrading and dangerous conditions of urban existence anywhere in the world. They form the environment in which perhaps one-third of the urban population of developing countries spend more or less the whole of their lives. Increasingly they shape the lives, attitudes and behaviour of their inhabitants and influence – even dominate – the total environment of the cities in which they occur. They are found throughout the world under a variety of names: favelas in Brazil, barriadas in Peru, ranchos in Venezuela, gecekondu in Turkey, bidonvilles in French-speaking Africa.

Sometimes the term 'transitional settlement' is used to describe slums and shanty towns of this kind: not because their physical existence is temporary, for most of them are permanent; and not because their inhabitants are in transit, for many spend their whole lives there; but because they are settlements in which a process of economic and social change is taking place. The residents, who often arrive poor, illiterate, hungry and in search of a better life, are undergoing changes in attitude and behaviour – going through the process of becoming citizens. At the same time their physical surroundings are changing too: sometimes, unfortunately, for the worse, but not always so. For in a number of developing countries people living in transitional settlements have shown remarkable vigour and ingenuity in improving their living conditions in the face of enormous obstacles, including strong opposition from the authorities to the very existence of these settlements.

Thus in the developing countries, where urbanisation has its most dramatic impact, the rapid growth of urban populations is not taking place as a simple increase in the size and number of cities as we now know them. The fundamental changes occurring through the urbanisation process are as radical as they are dynamic, and the strongest and most effective forces shaping these cities of the future are those that result in the creation and growth of transitional settlements. In many developing countries the inhabitants of transitional settlements are rapidly becoming the majority of the population of urban areas. In some cities this is already the case. The United Nations Centre for Housing, Building and Planning recently assembled crude, but roughly comparable, figures for thirty-six cities in developing countries which support this contention.[8] Of these cities, only six had transitional settlement populations which formed less than 25 per cent of the total urban population. Half of them had transitional populations which formed a third or more of the urban population and in five cities transitional populations constituted an actual majority.

In Seoul, for example, 30 per cent of the dwellings in 1966 were classified as shacks, mostly occupied by two or more families. In Manila, more than 1.1 million out of approximately 3 million inhabitants live in slums and squatter settlements, and the squatter population alone increased from 360,000 in 1962 to 767,000 in 1968. In Dar es Salaam, in 1968, more than a third of the population of 273,000 was living in slums and squatter conditions. In Guayaquil in the same year 360,000 out of an estimated total population of 730,000 were living in squatter settlements. In Ankara it was estimated in 1970 that 60 per cent of the population were squatters.

In Morocco, an estimated 600,000 people — 4.5 per cent

of the national population — were living in bidonvilles in 1965. In Ghana it was estimated that in towns of 5000 to 50,000 inhabitants, 20 per cent were living twenty or more to a house: in three larger towns the figure was 35.6 per cent. The latest housing census in Iraq showed that only one-fifth of the total housing stock of 766,000 dwellings were made of durable materials; 40 per cent were made of mud and similar materials and about 25 per cent were made of reeds, tin cans, boards, canvas and other junk.

These figures mark only a point in time in a far from static situation. While the total population in developing countries tends to grow at 2 to 3 per cent annually and many city populations grow at 6 per cent or more annually, transitional settlements commonly grow by 12 per cent and in some cases by more than 20 per cent annually. At 12 per cent growth rate, a population doubles in less than seven years; at 20 per cent it doubles in four years. It is futile to expect or hope that this rapid growth can be stopped or even significantly slowed down. All the indications are that migration to urban areas will not only continue but will grow in force. Nor should governments of developing countries try to impede this process, for urban growth is both a basic condition and an inherent consequence of social and economic development. The success of population control policies and rural modernisation programmes is largely dependent on urbanisation and the development of urban attitudes.

The apparent sameness of all transitional settlements, with their makeshift houses and lack of ordinary facilities, hides a wide range of defects and disguises the fact that these places are usually either improving or getting worse. The chief environmental problems vary according to whether the settlement is a central slum whose population has been swollen by migrants and more rapid natural growth or a previously vacant site invaded and settled in some fashion outside the conventional framework of urban development. Conditions are also influenced by the length of time the settlement has been in existence, the circumstances under which it has grown, the physical characteristics of the site, the climate, the rate of economic growth of the city to which it is attached and the ability of the settlers to take part in its economic activity, their access to community services and facilities and the attitudes of all levels of public authority towards the existence of the settlement.

Whatever the local circumstances, the degree of environmental deprivation is likely to be severe. Access to water for drinking and household uses is usually difficult, irregular and expensive; and the water is often contaminated. There is usually no proper means of getting rid of human and household wastes, so they are allowed to accumulate and provide a fertile breeding ground for pests and vermin, and thus for disease. The houses are usually overcrowded, lack privacy and offer little protection from the extremes of weather. The settlement as a whole is likely to be densely populated and without open spaces. Fire is a constant and devastating hazard. There is usually little or no public transport to other parts of the city. There may be no health, education and recreation facilities in the settlement or close enough to be accessible. Sickness and infant mortality rates are usually high and life expectancy short. Whether the settlement is newly formed or many generations old, the majority of its inhabitants are likely to be young newcomers to the urban area. Their incomes are usually low and uncertain. The settlers, unable to escape from their immediate surroundings for any appreciable length of time, are liable to be more than usually influenced in their behaviour and attitudes by the nature of their surroundings. They may be frustrated and dissatisfied by their inability to take part more fully in urban life; that is to say they are disappointed in the expectations which drew them to the city in the first place.

Squatter settlements and environmentally deprived slum areas do of course occur in the developed world, but they are not such a critical problem there as they are in the developing world. Most developed nations have the necessary financial and technical resources to replace slums and squatter settlements by decent housing in appropriate locations. The decision to do so is largely a matter of political will. Developing countries do not have this choice. They must adopt a radically different approach which recognises the existence of transitional settlements and the vital role they have to play in the economic and social development of the nation.

Central City Problems

In developed countries the crucial issue of the urban environment is the problem of the central and inner areas of large cities, conurbations and metropolitan regions. Central city areas are at once the foci of the greatest conflicts within a wide diversity and complexity of interrelated land uses and human activities and the generators of environmental hazards which threaten both the health and safety of the citizens and the very ability of the city to function. At the same time such areas play a primary and vital role in the life of the city, the region, the nation and, in some cases, of the world. They may be the seat of government and the home of national and international organisations; the hub of urban, regional, national and international transport and communication networks; the focal point of commerce, industry, shopping, higher education and cultural institutions.

Characteristically, the central area is the oldest part of the city and has remained in the same location — possibly for centuries — while new uses and activities have been piled on and squeezed in by successive generations. Such areas are in a state of constant change, a continuous cycle of decay and regeneration in which some elements lag behind others. While the infrastructure of paved road and footpaths, electricity and water supply, sewerage and refuse disposal systems is usually complete, many of its components may be inadequate, obsolete or irrational. Similarly elements in the health, welfare, education and public protection services may be obsolete or inadequate. Under the impact of rapidly advancing technologies and increasing affluence, environmental conditions in many central city areas are generally deteriorating. Congestion on the roads and footpaths and in the public transport systems is increasing; air and water pollution, noise and litter are growing worse. Deteriorating environmental conditions, combined with overcrowded housing, unemployment and inadequate services and facilities, give rise to physical and mental illnesses, crime and vandalism.

The physical fabric is commonly a mixture of old and new,

often including a high concentration of historic buildings and monuments. Often individual buildings and even whole districts are put to a use other than that for which they were intended. Indeed the existence of cheap and obsolete property alongside the new may be vital to the generation of new activities and enterprises, which is one of the essential functions of a city centre, just as the coexistence of historic buildings and modern facilities is an essential part of the city's attraction for tourists and visitors.

The density of both buildings and people in central areas is usually high and the daytime population may be many times the resident population, being largely made up of commuting workers, shoppers, day visitors and tourists. The central core, containing the business, administrative, shopping and cultural quarters, together with the surrounding inner areas, may contain the greatest concentration within the urban area of obsolete and slum housing on the one hand and expensive luxury housing on the other. Thus the area is likely to provide homes for only the lowest and the highest paid, while the middle range must commute from the suburbs and surrounding towns and villages.

The population of the inner areas is often declining — that of Inner London, for instance, has been falling continuously for seventy years — and is liable to be unbalanced, with a preponderance of the old, the unmarried, the very poor, the badly educated and the immigrant. Most city centres are or have been reception areas for immigrants, offering them relatively low-cost housing and unskilled employment — often low-paid jobs in catering and public transport. Social segregation by race and income is often pronounced: the central area is traditionally the home of the ghetto.

The unique characteristics of city centres, setting them apart from suburbs and smaller towns, derive from their complex and concentrated economic, social and cultural functions; and therein lie their successes and their failures. Some of the specialised activities which take place in the city centre can only survive when they are accessible to a large number of people within a small area, yet this very concentration produces intense competition for land and severe congestion of people and vehicles. The more successful the centre and the more demand there is for its activities and services, the more people it attracts and the more difficult and unpleasant it becomes to reach the centre from outlying areas and to move around within it. Thus the continuing prosperity and viability of the centre are threatened.

The long-term trend of rising land prices, the obsolescence or inadequacy of public transport systems, the congestion in central streets, the introduction of new technologies and forms of organisation and the sheer growth of population in metropolitan areas have all combined to drive some traditional activities out of the city centres. Manufacturing, wholesale markets and warehousing, which require large ground areas, tend to move out to suburban or peripheral areas, accompanied by new housing for workers in these industries. A particularly striking example is provided by port activities, which used to be a traditional feature of many central areas and a large source of employment. Aided by the introduction of mechanised and automated handling, and particularly by the use of containers, many port users have abandoned city centres for peripheral areas. In most large cities central areas no longer provide maximum accessibility in terms of transport costs and journey times for goods and people. Improved road networks outside the city have given the advantage to suburban locations. Space vacated by manufacturing, warehousing and residential uses in central areas is most commonly taken over for office development, but in some cases offices too are moving to suburban centres.

Central cities are not generally without planning policies and controls, but the powers and resources of the local planning authorities and the areas over which they are exercised are often inadequate. The problems of the central city cannot be solved entirely within the city nor by the municipal authorities alone.

The Pull of Primate Cities

Uncontrolled population movements and unplanned urban growth tend to distort the pattern of settlements within a national territory. Before the present trend of rapid growth in the largest settlements became established there was in many countries a widespread network of towns of comparable size, all performing similar functions. More often than not they had come into being as local markets at natural focal points such as river crossings or junctions of trade routes. They acted as centres for small-scale manufacturing and as seats of local administration serving the surrounding areas. Under the influence of the industrial revolution and the advent of mechanised transport a number of places which offered a particularly advantageous location for trade and industry began to grow rapidly, outpacing the less favoured towns. In several South Asian and Latin American countries, but also in such developed countries as France and England, one city has thus become many times larger than any other in the country. The tendency for industry, services and the country's intellectual élite to concentrate in only one or two leading cities has also been marked in countries which until recently had a colonial or semi-colonial status.

Once a leading city has outdistanced others, its primacy tends to be increased further by all subsequent developments. Migratory streams are reinforced as country people head for the city where relatives and neighbours are already established. The existence of specialised industries and services in the primate city attracts and generates new investment there, while lack of such stimuli discourages investment and enterprise in smaller centres. Businessmen, managers and professional people are attracted to the leading city and are reluctant to stay in or move to smaller centres with fewer facilities and opportunities. The modern attitudes and technologies which flow from large cities, while essential to national growth, often endanger the livelihood of rural areas and small settlements and thereby further strengthen the dominance of the big city. Mechanised and automated processes in agriculture and industry, introduced to improve output, reduce the number of jobs available and undermine the livelihood of traditional craftsmen, who find their skills and their products no longer in demand. When this happens in rural areas and small towns where job opportunities are already limited, more people are forced to migrate. In developing countries the spread of urban attitudes by elementary education, the cinema and radio also encourages migration by making people dissatisfied with rural and small-town life. The provision of roads and public transport where none existed before may also encourage migration by making it easier.

These trends rob small towns of their vitality and at the same time overburden the leading city by a too rapid increase in population, which outruns the city's ability to provide jobs, houses, public utilities, education and health and welfare services. They have their most dramatic impact in developing countries, which lack the resources and mechanisms for dealing with the problem, but they are apparent also in modified and complex forms in more developed countries. In developed countries too a counter-trend is upsetting the efficient functioning of overgrown metropolitan areas. Here the outflow of people and of industrial and commercial activities from central cities to administratively independent suburbs and satellite towns is weakening the ability of the central city to carry out its vital economic, social and cultural role in the region and the nation. The loss of local tax income hinders essential redevelopment and modernisation and reduces the ability of the municipal authorites to meet the needs both of the poor and socially deprived people who still live in central areas and of the commuters who daily make use of the city's roads, public transport and civic amenities.

Conflicts in the Settled Environment
Distortion of the national network of settlements is one of the main consequences of unplanned urban growth. The other main consequence which concerns us here is its effect on the environment of individual settlements.

The settled environment is a complex mixture of natural and man-made elements which interact with each other. This is true whether or not the settlement is planned. In the unplanned settlement, however, the relationship tends to be one of conflict. (One of the principal objectives of physical planning is to ensure that as far as possible the relationship is harmonious and the total effect is beneficial.) The quality of the environment is further influenced by the activities which take place within the settlement, while the efficiency with which the activities are performed is in turn influenced by the environment. Here again the process of interaction cannot be avoided but can be controlled.

One of the basic changes in the natural environment brought about by large settlements involves the climate. The shape of the buildings, their heat-retaining properties and the heat-generating activities which take place within them combine to create a micro-climate which is quite distinct from that of the surrounding area. In general, strong winds are decelerated and light winds are accelerated as they move into towns; the chemical composition of the air is changed; radiation gains and losses are both reduced; temperatures are substantially raised; fogs are thicker, more frequent and more persistent; visibility is reduced; and rainfall is sometimes increased.

There is a complex relationship between the local climate of a settlement and the various forms of air pollution produced by the settlement. The waste heat, gases and other pollutants released into the air help to shape the climate, while the climate in turn influences the extent to which these pollutants remain concentrated over the city or are dispersed into the wider atmosphere. The shroud of pollution over a city affects the way the sun's rays reach the ground: studies have shown that short-wave radiation can be reduced by up to one-fifth. In badly polluted areas half the visible radiation and four-fifths of the ultra-violet radiation can be lost. London's campaign to stop smoke pollution from domestic fires and industrial and commercial furnaces has not only resulted in cleaner air but has also increased the average amount of winter sunshine by 50 per cent compared with the situation before the passing of the Clean Air Act in 1956. This increase in sunshine is not only welcome in itself: by increasing surface temperatures it has strengthened air turbulence and thereby helped to reduce the concentration of sulphur dioxide.

High temperatures are not always welcome, of course. Throughout much of the central and eastern United States prolonged periods of hot and humid weather during the summer are associated with higher-than-average death rates, particularly among the elderly and the infirm. These 'heat deaths' are most prevalent in large urban areas, where night-time temperatures are often several degrees higher than in nearby rural areas.

The blanket of warm air over cities also tends to increase rainfall — by about 10 per cent compared with nearby open country. On the other hand it can result in less snow, since snowflakes sometimes thaw as they fall through the warm air and lying snow tends to melt more quickly than in open country.

Air flow is another important element in this complex system of interrelationships between settlements and their local climate. Good air flows help to disperse pollution. On the other hand air turbulence caused by large tall buildings can be dangerous to the buildings and can make life intolerable for people on the ground.

The severity of air pollution in urban areas depends, of course, not only on the local climate but also on the number, kind and concentration of pollution sources — domestic fires and central-heating furnaces, power stations, industrial processes, transport. The pollutants arising from these sources include sulphur oxides, nitrogen oxides, carbon monoxide, soot, metals, dust and grit. They do clearly defined damage to vegetation and buildings and they are known to have adverse effects on human health.

Smoke and sulphur dioxide from burning coal have been associated with an above-average number of deaths in large cities on occasions when freak weather has prevented these pollutants from dispersing and thus caused smog. Those who die are generally the very young, the old and people suffering from cardiac and respiratory diseases, and it is reasonable to suppose that a high proportion of the deaths are due to irritation of the respiratory tract. These acute effects in times of exceptional pollution must be distinguished from sub-acute and suspected chronic effects of lesser, everyday concentrations. The sub-acute effects show as increases in illness which accompany or closely follow minor increases in pollution in large towns. 'Normal' air pollution is suspected of helping to cause chronic bronchitis and lung cancer. In the absence of conclusive proof of these chronic effects atmospheric pollution by sulphur oxides is often allowed to continue unabated. But the success of London's clean air campaign and of the rebuilt Warsaw's central thermo-electric plants shows that it is feasible to reduce pollution from heating sources.

The largest and gravest source of air pollution in many areas is the motor car. The petrol engine emits carbon monoxide and unburnt hydrocarbons, nitric oxides and fuel additives such as lead. In busy city streets carbon monoxide may reach concentrations well above those permitted in industry, most of it coming from motor vehicles. In the United States, 60 per cent of carbon monoxide air pollution is caused by motor vehicles: in Washington D.C., a non-industrial area, the figure is 80 per cent. Recent legislation in the United States to control motor vehicle emissions should, by 1975, have a major impact on air pollution. Pioneering efforts have been made in this direction in Los Angeles, where the introduction of emission control devices has already reduced the level of hydrocarbons and carbon monoxide even though the number of cars has increased.

Motor vehicles are also a major source of noise, along with aircraft and other forms of transport, industry and construction work. Excessive noise has a fairly well established effect on health, although it tends to receive less attention than air pollution and is subject to far fewer controls. Investigators have associated noise with hypertension, the increase in diseases of the central nervous system, deafness, tiredness, reduced capacity to work and insomnia. The human ear cannot hear all sounds and not all people can hear the same sounds. The average normal adult of twenty-five to thirty years of age can hear sounds ranging from twenty to 20,000 cycles per second. As a person ages his hearing capacity tends to narrow and he may have difficulty hearing some sounds within that range. Some of these losses may be due to excessive noise or to prolonged exposure to noise of less intensity. But noise affects not only hearing but also other aspects of health through its effects on the nervous system. It has been shown that high frequency noises can lead to deterioration in the working of the brain, in the body's capacity to renew its own tissue and organs, and in the working of the internal secretion glands. Low frequency noises can produce progressive slowing down of reflexes in the central nervous system.

The effects on the body are never simply those of noise

itself but of noise in association with other factors, chemical, physical, mental and biological. It is clear that the nervous system's resistance to noise is lessened by physical and mental illness, and that changes in the body's biological rhythm brought about by, say, night work affect man's resistance to noise. A prolonged excess of noise induces defective working of the cardiovascular and digestive systems, leading to arteriosclerosis, hypertension, stomach ulcers and so on. Hypersensitivity to noise has been noted in women during the pre-menstrual phase, at the end of pregnancy and during the menopause.

It is not easy to establish a correlation between the increase of noise, which is objective and measurable, and the increase of the disturbance it causes, which is subjective and not so easily assessed. The reaction of people to noise is complex and variable, depending on such factors as health, age and occupation. In addition sounds have several characteristics, such as intensity (loudness) and wave frequency (pitch or tone), which together with variations in their incidence (suddenness, repetition, duration) have to be taken into account in determining their effects. Most current studies are restricted to the analysis of the disturbance caused by different noise intensity levels on the human organism.

Perhaps the greatest objection to air pollution and noise is that their total health implications are unknown. The effects of some pollutants or combinations of pollutants may not become fully apparent for generations. Increasing respect for unknown health hazards has recently sprung from a growing awareness that research often refutes conventional wisdom. By way of illustration we may note reactions to the supersonic aircraft which are now being tested. The argument that nitric oxide from the exhausts of supersonic transports could damage the protective ozone layer of the atmosphere was at first dismissed by experts. However, a leading authority, Dr. Harold Johnston of the University of California at Berkeley, has recently claimed that 500 supersonic aircraft operating seven hours a day would cut the ozone content of the atmosphere in half in less than a year. Since the ozone layer protects the earth from lethal ultraviolet rays, world-wide blindness would follow. This predic-

tion has, of course, been questioned but it is indicative of the more cautious and circumspect attitudes towards the environment which now exist.

Liquid and Solid Wastes

Settlements produce large and increasing amounts of human, animal and other organic liquid and solid wastes and industrial wastes which, if not properly removed and disposed of, pose a dangerous threat to health and to the environment. The connection between contaminated water sources and major gastro-intestinal infections was established in London 120 years ago. Since then much has been learnt about sewage disposal and treatment and the protection of water sources and supplies, and in the developed world cholera, typhoid and paratyphoid fever and a host of water-borne diseases have been more or less eradicated. However, conditions very much like those which prevailed in Europe in the middle of the nineteenth century when these problems began to receive attention can be found today in many urban areas of the developing world where faecal pollution of water systems is commonplace. Here, gastro-intestinal disorders are endemic and cholera epidemics frequent.

Sewage does not only contaminate public water supplies. It also runs over the ground where children play and into pools and streams where they bathe, exposing them to serious parasitic diseases. It comes into contact with fruit and vegetables where they grow and in the markets; with milk on dairy farms; with meat in abattoirs and shops; with food handlers and utensils.

Even where sewage is safely removed from buildings and the immediate area of settlements by sewerage systems it is often poured with little or no treatment into rivers, lakes and seas close to settlements. Effluents from manufacturing industry and food processing, containing organic compounds and trace metals, are also discharged directly into water courses. The 'death' of the Great Lakes and the catastrophic decline in the water quality of the Rhine are among the most spectacular examples of what can happen. On the other hand, London's reclamation of the Thames, where fish are now returning for the first time in a century, illustrates how this trend can be reversed.

The increased production of wastes of all kinds is one of the inevitable consequences of economic development and urban growth. In fact the amount of goods a society consumes can be measured just as well by the wastes it produces as by the money it spends. Growing affluence brings not only an increase in the amount of waste but also a change in its composition. The problems of treatment and disposal have been particularly aggravated by the increasing use of wrapping materials which vastly augment the bulk of solid waste without increasing its weight to anything like the same extent. Even so it is estimated that the weight per head of domestic refuse in some metropolitan areas has almost doubled in the past twenty-five years.

The refuse problem is particularly serious in the rapidly growing cities of the developing world where the municipal authorities cannot keep up with the tremendous amount of waste produced. Refuse left uncollected or dumped without proper treatment pollutes water and soil and attracts vermin and insects, thereby breeding disease. Everywhere the growing volume of refuse is bringing difficulties in collection, transportation and disposal. Increasing amounts of land at increasing distances from cities are being taken up for refuse tips. Incineration, which often appears an attractive alternative to tipping, causes air pollution.

Mental Health
The modern urban environment and life-style it induces seem to take their toll in mental illness, aberration and anti-social behaviour, although it is even more difficult — and controversial — to find a direct cause-and-effect relationship in this area than between air pollution and ill-health. A number of studies have shown that the incidence of schizophrenia is greater in the central areas of large cities and diminishes towards the outskirts. There are two schools of thought about why this should be so: the first argues that social factors, including 'social isolation' breed mental illness; the second maintains that central areas attract unstable people who seek the anonymity and lack of social constraints found there.

Attempts have been made to explain mental disorders as symptomatic of the social stresses experienced by city people and two of these studies are outlined below. However, it should be noted that most practitioners schooled in biological psychiatry question the possibility of establishing a correlation between the prevalence and incidence of mental disorders and the social factors which some sociologists suspect of causing them.

A study of schizophrenia published by E. H. Hare[9] in 1960 analysed 441 cases admitted to the mental hospital in Bristol, England, over a five-year period. Hare concluded that the person who became schizophrenic was often a 'difficult personality' who was rejected by the family and therefore left home and moved to the city centre where lodgings were easier to find. The ensuing isolation, he suggested, might then open the way to schizophrenia.

Another study of the supposed relationship between mental illness and the urban environment was carried out by G. D. Klee[10] and others in an area of Baltimore, U.S.A., known as 'the Block', which in 1960 had a population of about 1400. Over a three-year period this area had an annual crime rate of 48 arrests for every 100 adults, a tuberculosis incidence of one in 100 and a psychiatric admission rate of 11 in 100. The authors concluded that there was much evidence that the true rates for many psychiatric disorders were substantially higher for people at the lower socio-economic levels and that 'as expected' there was a positive association between psychiatric admission rates and over-crowding.

With some exceptions, the data showed that areas which ranked high for poverty, social disorganisation and certain public health problems tended to have high total psychiatric rates. The findings at least underlined the need for a broad preventative approach to psychiatric problems and a unified service for medical, psychiatric and social ills. The authors said 'While this concept has long had wide currency, its application is negligible. We look forward to truly comprehensive programmes of community mental health, public health and social rehabilitation based on ecological orientation.'

Studies carried out in a number of countries suggest that

there may be a higher incidence of mental illness among migrants in urban areas, arising from the stresses and strains of a new and possibly bewildering environment, loss of contact with family and friends and a sense of loneliness, isolation and neglect. Migrants are mostly young people and most of them are poor, unskilled and, in many countries, illiterate or poorly educated. Many find themselves no longer subject to family or tribal protection and restraint. More generally, among many young people in many large cities poverty, unemployment and a poor environment may lead to delinquency, drug addiction, alcoholism, prostitution, venereal diseases, crime and anti-social behaviour.

3 A Comprehensive Approach

Conventional Responses to Urban Problems
Two things should now be abundantly clear. Firstly, that the population of the world is growing fast and changing its pattern of distribution on the face of the earth. Secondly, that a large proportion of the world's population is already living in conditions and surroundings that are unsatisfactory either through poverty and lack of basic amenities or through the adverse side-effects of affluence and advanced technologies. From these two inescapable facts we can draw only this conclusion: we must increase our capacity to feed, house and employ ourselves and meet our other fundamental needs and at the same time reduce the detrimental effects of these activities on our environment. We must do both these things together because a deteriorating environment is not just unpleasant; it affects our very capacity to survive and prosper.

Many conventional responses to the problems brought by growth and shifts in population only make the environmental situation worse or achieve a short-term benefit at the cost of creating longer-term problems. We only have to look at the conventional reaction to the transitional settlements which form such a large, growing and dominant part of cities in the developing world. Often these areas are simply ignored by the authorities. Often they are passively opposed without steps being taken either to ameliorate them or to provide settlers with an alternative to crowding into overcrowded slums or building makeshift houses on vacant land. Occasionally the severity of the environmental problems provokes the authorities into sporadic actions which do not take into account the circumstances which cause such areas to develop and do little or nothing to improve the situation of the settlers.

What usually happens in these cases is that the settlers are expelled and the bulldozers are sent in to clear the land. If nothing is done to provide the squatters with alternative accommodation they are simply forced to start again somewhere else. If something is done the results may be little better. For when the authorities in developing countries attempt public housing schemes they often try to follow the pattern set in more developed countries. Complete houses are built — usually, it is true, providing only minimal standards of space and amenity. But even at these standards the houses are too expensive for the slender and uncertain means of the squatters and others at the bottom of the socio-economic ladder, especially if rents are set high enough to cover the investment. Thus they remain beyond the reach of the people for whom they are intended. At the same time they represent, in terms of the results achieved, a wasteful use of scarce national or municipal resources. Clearly this approach offers no solution to the problems of the rapidly growing transitional settlements. Even if it were economically feasible it might still be the wrong answer, for high-quality housing may be far from the top of the settler's list of priorities.

Given a rapidly increasing population and the poverty, absence of facilities and lack of opportunities in rural areas, the continued growth of these transitional settlements in is inevitable. The question is whether their future growth must mirror the environmental deprivation and human misery hitherto associated with these areas. Fortunately there is reason to believe that transitional areas can be converted into a positive element in national economic and social development. As we have noted in the previous chapter, in a number of developing countries people living in such areas have shown a remarkable vigour and ingenuity in improving their living conditions in spite of enormous obstacles, including the opposition of the authorities to the very existence of their settlements. All the current evidence from the developing countries suggests that when squatters obtain minimally secure employment and a measure of security in their tenure of the land they occupy they set about improving their homes and surroundings by their own efforts and with their own resources. In a number of cities transitional settlements have evolved in this way to become a significant social and economic asset to the community and the nation, at little or no expense to the government.

It is the potential and actual will of the people living in these settlements to improve their economic, social and physical circumstances that holds out so much hope for themselves and their countries. But this driving force must be recognised, encouraged and helped if it is to be harnessed. The development of policies and programmes to improve the environment of cities of which transitional areas form a significant and increasing part must depend upon an under-standing of the forces which bring them into being, a recognition of the human rights of their inhabitants and support for the process of progressive improvement. Govern-ments should seek to identify and remove the barriers to such improvement and act to help the process by providing services which the people cannot provide themselves. A solution on these lines is discussed in more detail in Chapter 5.

Transitional settlements demand a high priority because their problems relate to so many people and cannot be solved easily or quickly. The inadequacy of the resources available to the governments of the developing countries precludes the adoption of massive crash programmes. In most cases the effects of positive government intervention will only be felt over the medium and long term. But the programme is so urgent that a whole-hearted commitment to its solution is needed now. Within four to six years, the shortest period within which new policies and programmes could become operative on an effective scale, many of these settlements will have doubled their population.

But transitional settlements are not the only case in which generally accepted solutions to the problem of housing people are not contributing as well as they might to the protection and improvement of the environment. The con-ventional housing system has its shortcomings too. In most countries the location of housing is a haphazard affair because it depends upon a host of public and private decisions taken without reference to urban growth policies or environmental criteria. House-building which does not take place within the framework of a comprehensive development plan can lead to the destruction of fine landscape, the pollution of waterways, the creation of unnecessarily heavy traffic flows and the need for an uneconomic provision of public utilities, services and facilities.

Housing lies second after agriculture in the amount of land it consumes. Unless adequate measures are taken to bring order to the processes of choosing locations and assembling plots of land for housing they will continue to threaten the satisfactory development of settlements and systems of settlements. The sheer scale of the housing need is daunting. It has been estimated that before the end of this century between 1100 million and 1400 million new housing units will be needed in the world. Assuming a medium estimate of 1250 million, an average annual output of more than 40 million new houses is required, about 10 million in the developed countries and 30 million in the developing countries. This represents ten new houses for every 1000 people. In the developing countries the present performance averages only two or three new houses for every 1000 people.

Probably most of the people in the world today still live in houses of mud, clay, bamboo or other locally available, easily obtained material. But as expectations rise they will demand the materials used by more advanced societies: they will want houses of steel, concrete, glass and plastics. The impact on the world's resources of building 1000 million houses in a period of thirty to fifty years has never been analysed and stands in need of internationally sponsored and supported research. The location of stone quarries and clay, gravel and sand pits, the way these resources are won and the condition the land is left in after the deposit is worked out are all critical environmental factors.

The construction and building-materials industries in developing countries are generally underdeveloped. Many materials have to be imported and this adds to foreign exchange problems and increases the cost of building. While there is no shortage of potential labour, the building industry's capacity to absorb and train unskilled men is limited by the number of managers and skilled workers. The problems of developing and maintaining the industry in a viable form are greater in the absence of national long-term building programmes, for it is especially vulnerable to peaks and troughs of demand, which hinder it from maintaining a stable labour force, organising on a large scale and introducing better technologies.

In most developing countries even minimal investment in housing has been neglected in the past in favour of investment in other, more obviously productive, sectors. Yet in some of these countries there is now a clear danger that slums and squatter areas may engulf existing cities before normal municipal services can be provided for the inhabitants. Major new efforts are needed, not only to define housing policies, goals and standards related to the need, but also to overhaul the entire system of housing finance, production and maintenance. This will involve greater emphasis on the marshalling of resources on a large scale through public authorities, co-operatives and housing corporations capable of assembling land, financing and carrying out developments and managing entire new towns or large city districts designated for improvement.

Houses cannot be seen simply as buildings. They need water and electricity supplies, sewerage systems and roads; the people living in them need community services and facilities. To take an extreme example, it is estimated that in the United States every additional 1000 people in a metropolitan area need 4.8 elementary school rooms, 3.6 high school rooms and 8.8 acres of land for schools, parks and playgrounds; 100,000 gallons of water and the treatment of 170 lbs of organic water pollutants a day; 1.8 policemen, 1.5 firemen, 1 hospital bed, 1000 library books and a fraction of a gaol cell.

Housing policies and programmes must also be related to national policies for urban growth and for the distribution of settlements. Housing must be provided as part of a comprehensive strategy of urban development covering both physical facilities and community services. The amount and location of housing must be related to the amount and location of the other elements in the urban community: jobs, shops, schools, hospitals, clinics, libraries, places of recreation and resort.

Health Aspects of Planning

It is particularly important that the planning of housing and other elements of a human settlement should be grounded in health considerations and closely co-ordinated with health programmes. Health — which the World Health Organisation defines as a state of complete physical, mental and social well-being — is a fundamental need and it is clearly related to the physical environment. A conference on metropolitan planning and development in Stockholm in 1961 sponsored by the United Nations and the Swedish Government in co-operation with the International Labour Organisation, the United Nations Educational, Scientific and Cultural Organisation and the World Health Organisation, agreed that the primary objectives of environmental health in urban areas were: (a) prevention and control of the transmission of infectious agents; (b) freedom from chemical hazards; (c) freedom from physical hazards; (d) freedom from stress that causes, or may cause, undesirable conditions; (e) promotion or enhancement of physical well-being; and (f) promotion or enhancement of social well-being.

The conference also recommended that health administrators and technicians should participate in the physical and general planning of urban and metropolitan areas from the earliest stages, and should be adequately represented in the departments in charge of such areas' planning and development policies. Traditionally, health planning and urban planning have tended to go their own ways, largely because they have been separately organised and have called upon different skills. Health planning has been concerned with eradicating ill-health while physical planning has been concerned with the improvement of the fabric of settlements. Increasingly, both kinds of planning are seen to be concerned broadly with human well-being and the quality of life. Physical planning no longer deals solely with urban forms, the layout of roads and the juxtaposition of buildings; more important, it no longer deals solely with the physical use of land. In one sense planning has always recognised that land is not used by buildings but by human activities, but what distinguishes modern urban planning is its direct and express concern with human activities, needs and aspirations. The implicit aim of improving social well-being has become explicit.

City Planning
In addition to the problems of providing new houses, infrastructure and services to cope with a growing population, most large urban areas face the problem of renewing and replacing worn-out buildings and obsolete street patterns in their central areas. Commonly this is done by the technique of urban renewal: that is to say, by the assembly of enough individual sites to form an area which can be redeveloped as a whole in such a way as to produce a more rational pattern of land use and a more efficient system of routes for pedestrians and vehicles. Urban renewal schemes have often been less successful than they should have been in improving the economic and social well-being of cities, largely because of a failure to involve the people affected in the plan-making process. But a new, more carefully considered approach is now emerging, characterised by the rehabilitation of existing buildings and the discriminating insertion of new buildings and facilities to maintain good neighbourhood patterns and life-styles.

In the cities of the developed world some of the severest environmental conflicts arise from the ever-increasing use of motor vehicles. As we have seen, petrol and diesel engines are a major source of air pollution. This pollution is increased, while journeys are delayed and life is made hazardous and unpleasant for pedestrians, when motor vehicles overtax the capacity of roads which were not designed to take the volume and type of traffic now attempting to use them. But the construction of bigger and better roads and parking places takes up an enormous amount of land, reducing the space available for other activities and destroying the urban fabric; and however much additional road and parking space is provided it never seems to keep up with the demand. Short-term relief is sometimes obtained by traffic management schemes which attempt to restrict the number of vehicles using urban roads, to restrict some roads or road lanes to specific kinds of vehicle — buses for instance — and to make the best use of available road space by introducing one-way systems. Long-term improvements, however, can only come through the optimal use of public transport systems and the deliberately ordered arrangement of land uses and transport routes.

The way in which industrial, residential and shopping areas and other urban functions are related to one another can increase or decrease the amount of travel that is necessary. The location of manufacturing industry and warehousing close to docks, rail terminals and highway interchanges can reduce the amount of goods traffic and keep goods vehicles out of residential and shopping areas. The provision of well-placed sub-centres can reduce the need to travel into the city centre, where traffic congestion and the conflicts it brings are usually most acute. (In Warsaw, for instance, journeys to the central area account for 55.5 per cent of all passengers carried by public transport and 75 per cent of all vehicular traffic.) An essential part of comprehensive urban planning is, therefore, the analysis of road networks and land-use patterns within the city and the region, and the prediction of the future land-use demands and traffic they are likely to generate.

Town-planning theory offers two basic models commonly used in planning the development of large towns: the concentric and the linear. The first is based on limiting the growth of the city and hiving off further development to a group of satellite towns. The second depends upon curtailing further expansion in some directions and channelling growth along chosen lines related to the basic pattern of roads and infrastructures. In either case the plan is likely to include the organisation of a hierarchy of centres. The master plan for Warsaw, for example, is based on a four-level system of centres. The first or lowest level provides everyday services for a neighbourhood or collection of housing estates with about 10,000 inhabitants. The second groups (for a catchment area of about 50,000 people) district services likely to be needed every few days. The third serves a group of districts containing 200,000 to 400,000 people, while the top level is the city centre serving the whole region and, for some services, the whole country. A proper allocation of functions throughout the four levels of the system allows the city centre to be relieved of activities which do not need to be centrally located, so that its limited space can be devoted to what are essentially city-centre functions.

Influencing Migration Patterns

In present circumstances continued urban growth is inevitable. In developing countries at least it is also necessary, for it forms an essential part of national economic and social development. This does not mean that there has to be continued growth of the existing large urban concentrations, for, as we have seen, when cities grow too fast they invariably suffer environmental degradation. Too much pressure is put on the existing infrastructure and services, which cannot be expanded fast enough to cope with the growing number of people. This is particularly true of developing countries, where, generally speaking, the pace of urban growth is far outstripping the pace of industrialisation, with the result that there are not enough jobs to employ the urban population and not enough wealth to support the expansion of physical facilities and services.

Another relevant aspect of the current pattern of urban growth in developing countries is the wide divergence in standards of living between urban and rural areas. The life-style and living standards of the villagers, peasants and small land-owners who make up the bulk of the rural population is often decades — even centuries — behind that of at least the more fortunate city dwellers and perhaps even of the less fortunate ones. Expectation of a better standard of living is one of the chief factors stimulating the endless flow of migrants from rural to urban areas in developing countries. If to the casual observer these migrants do not appear to be much better off in their slums and shanty towns, they themselves believe they are. They are not, in any case, discouraged from migrating by the conditions they find in the cities. The difference in living standards also leads to tensions and political instability in rural areas. Yet often little is being done to redress the balance. Public investment tends to be concentrated in urban areas, partly as a matter of prestige and partly as the result of political pressures, even where most of the country's foreign currency is earned by the export of agricultural products.

The economic and environmental problems found in cities and those which prevail in rural areas may stem from somewhat different causes, but both point towards the same solution: a wider distribution of urban settlements and investments throughout the national territory.

Any attempt to influence population distribution must be rooted in an overall development policy operating at both national and regional levels. There are enough examples of countries that have adopted decentralisation policies and have introduced, at considerable costs, special incentives for firms and individuals to move to development areas, only to find their efforts wasted as growth continues unabated in the same areas as before. There have been cases, on the other hand, where population distribution policies, pursued as integral parts of national development plans and supported by the vesting of authority in planning agencies, have significantly modified previous population trends.

It is rarely possible or desirable to control migration patterns directly, although measures have been and are being taken in some countries to return migrants to rural areas. Such a policy requires strong controls, including the registration of all inhabitants and the issue of passports or work permits. It has been used in China, where a 'blind migration' of rural workers was met by their identification and eviction from the cities and by measures to reintegrate them into the rural economy. It is practised in South Africa, where Africans in the cities are compelled, after a period of permitted urban residence, to return to their rural places of origin. The system also compels African city workers to live in specific townships.

The more usual practice, however, is to influence population movements indirectly by manipulating a number of variables, notably the location of industry and the provision of infrastructure, which work together to increase the appeal of areas where the government wishes to retain or attract population. A number of distinctive policies — rural development, new town development, 'growth poles' — can be applied singly or in combination.

Rural Development

Rural development programmes should not be undertaken in the belief that they will alleviate urban ills by reversing the urbanisation process. There is little to suggest that any government has succeeded to a measurable degree in slowing down urban growth. But rural development can help to smooth the transition between rural and urban life, and to narrow the gap between them in living standards, by disseminating urban attitudes, providing job opportunities and introducing education, health and welfare services, public utilities and communal facilities. It can also provide city people with the pleasure of access to the countryside for recreation.

A rural development programme should, therefore, form part of the population distribution policy of any developing country. But in many countries rural development – or development in rural areas, which is not necessarily the same thing – is carried out without sufficient regard for its impact on the rural settlement system or the local economy. Often technical aspects and national economic considerations take precedence over human and environmental considerations. Typical of this approach are the major river-basin development projects in which emphasis is placed on water storage and hydro-electric power generation while the effect on local people's way of life is treated in a cursory manner. In agriculture, the Green Revolution can bring drastic changes in the rural economy, with the mechanisation of farming displacing workers and reinforcing the flow of migrants to the cities. There are conflicts here which are difficult to resolve between the very proper and necessary goal of increasing production and the equally important goal of retaining rural employment.

These problems tend to arise because of the narrow approach of government departments and agencies with specific responsibilities, operating without any machinery to co-ordinate their aims and means. In some cases agricultural departments may be carrying out soil surveys and land-use studies while some other agency, concerned with, say, the exploitation of mineral resources, may be formulating incompatible proposals for the same area. In many countries welfare agencies are promoting the building of minor roads by local communities on a self-help basis while arterial roads are being built by public works agencies, with each type of agency ignoring the effects of its activities on the other's programme.

An effective rural development policy is one which increases the opportunities for employment by, for instance, the introduction of intensive agriculture, factories for processing agricultural products and workshops for repairing agricultural implements, and at the same time brings the benefit of health, education and welfare services to rural settlements. Such a policy may well involve the consolidation of fragmentary land-holdings and a more equitable and rational redistribution of land. The objective will be to create larger settlements where small industries and community services can be economically operated. Selected villages will be turned into district centres serving a group of villages and attracting, by their enhanced job opportunities, migrants who might otherwise move to large cities. An essential part of village development in this context is the provision of adequate water supplies and sanitary arrangements, both to increase the attraction of the selected villages and to reduce the risk of environmental degradation, which would otherwise become more acute with the increase in their size.

All this points to the need for a comprehensive approach to rural development to create a framework within which its benefits can be maximised and its social costs minimised. At present such an approach is rare. There are only a few instances where rural settlements have been planned with the simultaneous consideration of the social, economic, environmental and administrative implications. A comprehensive plan for rural development should be concerned with improving the overall standard of living and environmental condition, as well as with closing the gap between rural and urban life by accelerating the pace at which an urban-rural continuum is formed. The objective does not have to be the elusive goal of stopping once and for all the stream of migrants from rural to urban areas. Rather it should be to broaden the economic base of rural areas so as to make them more attractive places in which to live and work. In particular the development plan should ensure that rural areas are no longer associated solely with agriculture. This is not to deny that agricultural development is a vital part of the process; indeed agriculture will still rank as the main base for rural prosperity; but it should be balanced by wider and more diverse job opportunities.

Comprehensive rural development planning should be organised on a regional basis. The national level on the one hand, and the local community level on the other, offer too broad and too narrow a field for comprehensive planning to be effecitve. Central government must, of course, provide general guidelines, objectives and policies, but these must be co-ordinated and turned into detailed plans at the regional level. The making of the regional plan should include an assessment of the availability within the region of suitable growth centres and the formulation of a list of activities and services which should be concentrated in them. A subsequent programme of resettlement and growth-centre promotion, if this is the indicated strategy, should be carefully controlled so as not to disrupt the established way of life, for this would probably be counter-productive. The incentives offered to farmers to leave their existing landholdings and move to new or expanding settlements — such as opportunities for education, health and other community services — must be presented in an attractive way. For ultimately the move to a new area must be the free choice of the individual: he must be able to see that the advantages outweigh the disadvantages.

District or sub-regional centres, where services, facilities and basic infrastructure can be economically provided, form a vital part of any rural settlement system. Rural development programmes, including agrarian reforms, may be hindered if such centres are lacking. They also help to divert migratory flows away from overcrowded cities, since it is usually cheaper to meet basic needs and easier for migrants to adjust themselves to urban life-styles in places which are close to their original homes. Moreover, they can provide diversified job opportunities either on a permanent basis or, where the agricultural cycle leaves farmers idle for part of the year, on a seasonal basis. The growth of such centres may be stimulated by the establishment of industries based on the processing of agricultural products.

In Kenya, district centres serve populations of about 40,000 and areas of thirty to thirty-five square miles. They are often located at nodal points on the local road network ten to fifteen miles apart. They provide administration at the district officer level, a district court, police post, health centre, secondary school, community hall, postal service and shops. There are two lower levels in the rural settlement hierarchy: market centres (which usually have a dispensary and a secondary school, and in some cases a community hall and postal agency) serve about one-third of a district, while local centres serving populations of about 10,000 usually have a barter market, a primary school and sometimes a dispensary.[1]

In Israel the grass-roots unit is the Moshav, an organisation of 80 to 100 farming families. A community centre provides day to day services for five or six Moshavim within a radius of about three kilometres. Regional centres located about ten kilometres from the furthest community centres provide more specialised services and usually have non-farming work forces about equal in size to the farming community they serve.[2] This example is a good yardstick of the level of urban services that can be provided in an authentic rural setting.

There is probably no single optimum size in terms of either area or population for the various categories of village or district centre in this sort of programme. Different countries have experimented with different figures, and even if, in particular instances, the success of the policy can be ascribed to the right choice of size and area, such experience cannot be considered generally applicable. Each country or region must design its own pattern in the light of prevailing circumstances and tradition as well as in accordance with the desired objectives. One factor which affects the size and layout of individual settlements and needs to be determined locally is the size of the plot of land to be held by each farmer. Another is the maximum convenient distance between the village and the furthest field. Past experience suggests that 10 per cent of the working day can be taken as a reasonable amount of time to be spent on travelling.

Among peasants in Latin America a 10-hour working day appears to be common, indicating a 30-minute limit for the journey between settlement and place of work. The maximum distance is then indicated by the average travelling time.

The location of villages is another important matter to be taken into consideration. Many rural settlements in developing countries are dangerously exposed to landslide or flood, or too close to malarial swamps or other health hazards. The risk is not always fully appreciated, and in several countries new settlements are springing up spontaneously without any guidance on such matters, largely because the machinery is not there to give it. The lack of qualified staff is an acute problem in such areas. An illuminating example of how qualified staff can be trained to meet a specific need – and incidentally to yield longer-term benefits – is provided by the action taken by the Government of Ghana when it was faced with the enormous task of resettling all the farmers displaced by the Volta River Dam. With United Nations support, the Government set up a school to train technicians to help to plan the resettlement. Many of those who trained to technician standard became interested in careers as fully-fledged professional planners and the school now has a complete curriculum, filling a gap in this field.

New Towns and Growth Poles

Rural development policies may be combined in a national population dispersal plan with the building of new towns and the expansion and revitalisation of existing urban centres which have failed to keep pace with the growth of primate cities and metropolitan areas. The development of new towns to relieve congestion in existing conurbations and to slow their rate of growth is adopted policy in Great Britain, the Federal Republic of Germany, Poland, the Soviet Union and a number of other countries. Large new towns have been built throughout the Soviet Union; in Sweden also some satellite towns have been established. These new communities are designed to be relatively self-sufficient in respect of housing, employment and shopping centres. In Mexico, India and Venezuela industrial towns established near existing big cities have effectively diverted part of the migratory flow.

The promotion of 'growth poles' is an alternative or complementary approach, based on the view that big cities are more apt to attract industries than small towns. In this strategy new development is channelled to a number of selected regional cities. A good example is provided by France, where regional development is planned on this basis — largely with the intention of diverting growth from the Paris region. A policy of consolidating numerous existing industrial centres rather than permitting a few already large cities to absorb most of the industrial development is characteristic of countries with centrally planned economies. The Soviet Union, for instance, has fostered the rapid growth of a number of widely separated second-order cities.

The weak point in existing settlement networks varies from country to country: in some it may be at the level of second-order cities which can act as regional centres; in others it may be at the level of district centres in rural areas. A strategy for population redistribution and urban growth must take into account the need for — and the needs of — a full range of settlements: metropolitan areas, second-order cities, regional and sub-regional centres, market towns, villages and hamlets. Since the geographic, economic and other factors governing settlement development vary greatly from country to country, no uniform pattern can be applicable to them all. Similarly there is no universally valid optimum size or rate of growth for individual settlements: the concept is valid only in a relative sense. The optimum size for any specific settlement depends upon many variables, including strictly economic factors, geographic factors, social and political traditions and the values and objectives of the people who live there.

The development strategy should be based on a careful analysis of the actual and potential role of existing settlements and the need for settlements of particular scales in specific locations. Armed with this information, planners can direct development projects to the best places. Except in the smallest countries, development strategies designed to achieve a complete hierarchy of interrelated settlements are best organised on a regional basis.

It is recognised that most governments, particularly those

of developing countries striving to achieve economic growth, will find it difficult to formulate appropriate accounting systems by which to determine environmentally acceptable ranges of urban growth and population distribution. The international community could help here by providing specialist services and advice. Organisations like the United Nations, the development banks and research institutions could accumulate international experience which might help individual countries in their policy formulation.

Distribution of Industry

All regional development policies are likely to depend to a greater or lesser extent on the dispersal of industry from metropolitan areas and the promotion of industrial investment in new towns, growth centres, and so on. Legislation controlling the location of industry, the provision of government-owned industrial estates and a variety of financial incentives and penalties can be used to implement such a policy. It should be noted, however, that industries vary greatly in the extent to which they are amenable to decentralisation and in the extent to which they generate employment. Capital-intensive plants which employ a small labour force can actually create unemployment if they replace, or compete with, less mechanised or automated establishments manufacturing a similar product. Some firms, too, depend upon the external economies (including access to other specialised industries and services) which are provided only by an existing large industrial complex. This is particularly true of newly established firms which have not yet grown large enough to incorporate specialised services within their own structure. Provision should be made for the needs of such firms in the development and redevelopment plans of metropolitan areas. It is for this reason too that in small countries there is wisdom in allowing or encouraging one city to grow large enough to support specialised industrial enterprises and professional services.

The key criterion for evaluating individual investment decisions within an overall development policy should remain that of relative profitability, but we need new ways of making this calculation. In the past the bulk of development in most industrialised countries has been characterised by a crude and even brutal economic approach. Such an attitude views development in narrow sectoral terms, placing a premium on short-term benefits and costs and rarely considering broader societal consequences. When the basis for evaluating a decision is restricted to analysing the benefits and costs to the developer alone, environmental considerations are neglected. We need an approach which takes into account and evaluates the social costs of individual decisions and we need a means of assessing comprehensively their long-term consequences. To give an example, a firm which might by conventional criteria decide that the most profitable location for its enterprise was in a crowded metropolitan area might be led to take a different view if it were obliged to contribute through taxes to the cost of remedying the consequent environmental damage.

At present firms and individuals are rarely held accountable for the undesirable environmental side-effects of their activities — air and water pollution, road congestion and so on — the costs of which have to be borne by the community as a whole. As a result concentrations of investment, and therefore of population, can grow far beyond the point at which collective costs exceed collective benefits. The point at which the two are in equilibrium might be considered an economic-environmental break-even point and used as a basis for determining when population concentrations become excessive. This 'principle of taking into account the full spectrum of costs and benefits, including those which are normally disregarded, should be applied even though some of the costs and benefits are difficult to quantify.

In order to measure and evaluate the environmental consequences of investment decisions we must establish standards derived from the goals we wish to achieve. Standards may be regarded as shorthand devices for identifying desirable and unacceptable situations. The setting of standards always involves two elements: an objectively established element which identifies cause and effect and a value element which indicates the importance attached to the subject. The standard finally depends on how these two elements are combined. Many of the criteria by which we make judgements have not been converted into standards partly because of a lack of scientific knowledge and partly because no value has been set on the factor concerned. Standards do exist in relation to the quality of buildings and public health measures, but there are virtually none that deal with environmental quality. Admittedly some pollution standards are being adopted, but they represent only first steps towards the goal of improving the environment. Other standards are needed to control the size, spacing and density of buildings in order to ensure an acceptable micro-climate in terms of air currents, thermal exchanges and the dispersal of pollutants. The design standards of comprehensive urban planning, perhaps more than any other element in the process, codify and interrelate the technical and normative elements in the development of a settled environment.

Comprehensive Planning

A narrow sectoral approach to the problems of urban development is bound to increase the risks of environmental degradation and social inequality – the features which characterise so many settlements in the world today. A comprehensive planning approach, on the other hand, in-creases the probability that the undesirable side-effects and consequences of the development process will be avoided or at least kept to an acceptable minimum. We have sought to establish three reasons why it is urgently necessary to adopt this approach: firstly, throughout the world the growth of population is fastest in large settlements; secondly, the greatest and most significant environmental conflicts are concentrated in these settlements; and thirdly, urban growth is a vital instrument for achieving higher levels of human development.

There is no longer much doubt that the economic, social and environmental problems of our cities and towns are interrelated. Thus policies and programmes aimed only at solving particular problems may fail to achieve their object-ives, and may aggravate other problems, if they are not co-ordinated. What we are advocating here, therefore, is a process of comprehensive planning which is designed to achieve a total improvement in the environment by integra-ting various groups of policies and activities. We are not suggesting that existing policies should be replaced by ones solely concerned with the environment, but that awareness of the environmental consequences of various activities should inform and enhance policy-making, planning and decision-taking.

Comprehensive planning provides the machinery for integrating the three sectors of development — economic, social and physical — and their component areas of housing, health, industry, education, infrastructure, recreation and so on. It helps to establish common goals which set the context for co-ordinating individual actions. It provides a means of orchestrating the forces of change to achieve these goals. It permits an evaluation of the broad range of consequences associated with any change. It helps to allocate resources rationally and equitably among the various sectors. It links national, regional and local issues in a series of reciprocal relationships, and enables activities to be integrated over a geographical area determined by the nature of the problem to be solved. It produces plans for the long term (twenty to thirty years), medium term (five to ten years) and short term which are mutually consistent, but flexible enough to accommodate unexpected changes and to be refined in the light of new information.

Comprehensive planning provides a means of analysing how the many elements in a settlement relate to one another and how action to change one element reverberates through the whole system. One can see, for instance, how a decision on the location and density of a housing development influences and is influenced by water supply, sewerage and the location of jobs, schools, shops and so on. Similarly one can relate the decision to prohibit the discharge of sewage and other wastes into a river both to the provision of alternative means of disposal and to the opportunities for recreation presented by a clean river. By the nature of things different decisions of this kind are bound to be taken at different points in the governmental system: the housing issue may be decided by a local authority and the water resource question by a central government department. Yet they are obviously related. Only by comprehensive planning can the nature of the relationship be made clear and the weight to be attached to various relevant factors be determined.

At the national level, comprehensive planning is concerned with establishing a broad context within which all lesser-order plans can be formulated. It involves establishing a co-ordinated set of goals in the various sectors of national endeavour, indicating priorities, allocating resources in accordance with these priorities and co-ordinating sectoral policies and activities to ensure that conflicts are minimised and that all endeavours contribute to the achievement of all goals. By the use of comprehensive planning, governments can weight the goal of an enhanced environment against those of economic and social development. They should indicate in general terms how much value is to be placed on clean air, pure water, freedom from excessive noise and the conservation of landscape and of historically and aesthetically valuable buildings and monuments. In this respect they should specify the extent to which individual rights should be circumscribed in the interests of the greater common good, and the respective roles of the public and private sectors in achieving national goals.

Five major policy areas which should be covered by the national comprehensive plan can be distinguished.

1 *Sectoral Policies.* These include general policies for agriculture, natural resources, industrial development, population distribution, settlement networks, health, education, communications, traffic and transport systems. The political and administrative structuring of the country can also be included in this category.

2 *Areal Policies.* The designation of development areas, 'growth poles' and other special areas where the Government wishes to accelerate the rate of growth.

3 *Resource Allocation.* The distribution of financial and manpower resources among sectors and by area. Financial allocations by regional and local areas are particularly significant for the horizontal co-ordination of policies.

4 *Equalisation.* Policies aimed at securing the equality or equity of rights and duties; providing minimum standards of living in terms of housing, social security and services and a more equitable distribution of benefits and burdens. In this category fall policies affecting the basic rights of citizens in such matters as land ownership in relation to planning controls and development proposals.

5 *Control.* The exercise of control over decisions taken by regional and local authorities in order to ensure conformity with national policies and compliance with national standards, and to co-ordinate the activities of the various regions and localities.

Regional plans prepared within the context of the national plan should provide the machinery for the practical solution of the problems of industrial location, infrastructure development and settlement growth. In many countries (developed and developing) there is no effective planning machinery at this level. But the national plan is not, except in the smallest countries, an appropriate vehicle for deciding the specific location of major developments as it cannot take into account local problems and environmental issues. Local authorities, on the other hand, have no power to control activities outside their boundaries which have an important bearing on local issues. Regional planning permits the establishment of realistic local goals and provides a framework within which development projects of national and local significance can find their proper place.

The major issue for regional planning is the interrelationship between the various settlements of the region and between the settlements and the rural areas. The regional comprehensive plan should, therefore, decide the focal points for urban growth, the distribution of industry, the layout of infrastructure systems, the means of waste disposal, the location of large-scale recreational areas and open spaces and the scope for the protection of high-quality agricultural land. Regional planning introduces a spatial and territorial dimension into the planning process: it is the point at which policies and activities are tied to specific locations.

The five major policy areas also apply to the regional level.

1 *Sectoral Policies and Actions.* In this category are included policies for urban-rural relationships, migration and population distribution within the region, industrialisation and the distribution of housing, hospitals, health centres and schools, as well as regional plans for land use, communications and road networks. The actual provision of services and the construction of infrastructural and other works may be undertaken at this or the local level.

2 *Areal Policies and Actions.* At the regional level the definition of development areas, 'growth poles', and so on, may be further refined and integrated with physical planning policies.

3 *Allocation.* Ideally there should be considerable regional discretion in the allocation of financial resources between policy sectors and localities within the region, irrespective of whether national allocations are primarily based on sectors or on regions. In the latter case, however, there tends to be more room for regional discretion in allocating resources according to regionally-determined priorities.

4 *Equalisation.* This policy area is generally much less crucial at the regional level but may be of some significance, especially if the features of the region are markedly different from those of other parts of the country and therefore require deviation from national policies. This situation occurs quite often in developing countries but less often in advanced countries, where cultural, social and economic affairs have generally reached a high level of integration.

5 *Control.* Regional control should be exercised over decisions taken by local authorities to ensure their integration and compliance with regional policies and plans.

It is at the level of local comprehensive planning that all the sectoral policies are brought together and applied to particular problems and issues. Local plans must be prepared within the framework and in accordance with the guidelines provided by national and regional plans. Given these inputs, the task of comprehensive planning at this level is to design a staged programme of investments and their spatial distribution within the locality. Alternative proposals should be evaluated against the social, economic, biological and aesthetic needs of the population. The aim should be to integrate, and establish harmonious relationships among, the many different components of each settlement so that actions taken with respect to one element will not produce undesirable effects on the others. This involves designing a system that interrelates the economic activities of the settlement, including industry, commerce and services; residential areas, transport and communication systems; recreation and leisure-time activities; infrastructure networks; public housing finance; tax policy; social and health services; education; open spaces and aesthetic and cultural components. These elements should be related spatially while at the same time the intensity with which activities are carried out at their various locations should be controlled. Control of the location and density of activities, coupled with building regulations, provide the basis for harmonising man-made elements with the natural environment.

Some feel that to talk about comprehensive planning is largely an academic exercise because there are so many unknown and uncontrollable variables involved. But the alternative of incremental and fragmented decision-making is clearly less satisfactory. The sort of planning that was once thought comprehensive is now recognised as parochial because concern for the environment has added a whole new range of variables which must be taken into account when making policy decisions. Faced with the pressing problems of urban growth, overburdened facilities and a deteriorating environment, we have no choice but to attempt to order comprehensively the relationships between the components of settlements. We must use every tool, no matter what its stage of development, if we are to improve our chances of coping with the immense difficulties and designing a livable environment.

4 The Process of Implementation

A Programme of Reform

Urban growth need not in principle create a bad environment. Properly planned and controlled it should enhance, not detract from, environmental quality by relieving pressure on the countryside, by providing goods and services in quantity and diversity, and by presenting opportunities for new and attractive habitats and ways of life. Moreover, urbanisation is an essential element in national economic and social development. Only in urban concentrations can the economies of scale necessary for industrial development be achieved; only there can the services necessary for rapid social development be efficiently provided. It is therefore important, particularly for developing countries, that urban growth and the location of settlements should be planned as an integral part of economic and social development.

Most urban development problems of the past and the present can be put down to the inability or unwillingness of central and local authorities to intervene actively and comprehensively in the development process. Haphazard urban growth and the degradation of the urban environment are due mainly to the failure of the authorities to co-ordinate policies and programmes which bear upon the process. In many countries the existing machinery for policy formulation and co-ordination is inadequate and fails to make use of the available knowledge and experience in these fields.

A national planning programme for the development of settlements needs an integrated package of laws, economic and fiscal measures, administrative machinery and executive agencies. Although the most sophisticated and complex mechanisms for planning and managing the development process can only be achieved in the more advanced countries, significant progress in these directions can be made also by

73

developing countries. In fact only a few countries have adopted and put to effective use all the available techniques for guiding settlement development in accordance with clearly formulated national and regional policies. In these countries there exists a large body of knowledge based on experience and research which is available to those countries which are only just beginning to face the issues of urban development and environmental control. However, since these problems are complex and relatively new, and since the customs, institutions and requirements of each country differ, it will be largely up to each nation to establish its own system, with the help of other nations and the international community. This chapter offers, not a ready-made package, but a guide to the components which any system is likely to require to be fully effective.

Reform should begin at the top. At the national level machinery should be established for formulating policies in the various sectors which influence the growth of settlements and the quality of the environment. The most critical sectors involved are population growth and distribution, urbanisation, industrial location, transport, housing and rural development. Within the context of national policies a similar policy formulation process should take place at regional and local levels. A comprehensive planning system is needed to co-ordinate policy formulation, decision-making and the programming of development activities between the various sectors, between the various departments and agencies of central government, and between the different levels of government.

The responsibility for policy formulation at the national level rests with the executive arm of government. This should be assisted by a planning agency which can receive and integrate data from various departments and regions, evaluate alternatives and place a rational and consistent set of policies before the decision-makers for their approval. Policy formulation on the basis of a realistic appraisal of problems and resources is an essential prerequisite to the design and implementation of development programmes. It is particularly important for developing countries that they should get this process right because of their accelerated rate of change and their shortage of resources.

Few governments, unfortunately, carry out a conscious and organised process of policy formation and co-ordination for settlements growth and urbanisation based on the interaction of economic, social and environmental aims of development. National planning in most countries is dominated by, or restricted to, economic considerations. Most indicators of growth used by governments emphasise economic changes. Little thought is given to the interrelationship between, on the one hand, economic development programmes and projects and, on the other, urban growth and the quality of the environment both generally and in specific places. Environmental planning is often given low priority: usually it is confined to the internal spatial arrangements of urban areas and is not allowed to influence national and regional settlement systems or to play a part in the larger framework of national development. Most governments, in fact, tend to view urban growth as a natural by-product of change and development rather than as one of the instruments which ought to be used to achieve development goals. Indeed, few governments have formulated policies and plans for population distribution and urban growth either independent of or integrated with economic development plans. The need to consider the social and environmental consequences of development decisions is only beginning to be realised, and methods for incorporating such considerations into the planning and evaluation of development programmes and projects are only now being worked out.

The first step, therefore, may have to be an examination of current practices and machinery with a view to reform. Often in developing countries the current machinery and practices of government are either a hang-over from a previous colonial administration or an adaptation, at the personal whim of political leaders or administrators, of the model of an advanced country. Such systems are usually inappropriate to the social and economic realities of developing nations.

A number of specific deficiencies can be identified. There is rarely, at any level of government, machinery for policy formulation which involves the participation of all the relevant government departments. Frequently plan-making units are isolated from the elected officials who make important policy decisions and from the administrative and executive branches that carry them out. Often there is no machinery for measuring and assessing the performance of plans and policies in order to update and refine them. Often, too, there is no provision for incorporating contributions from outside bodies such as universities and interest groups and from the general public.

These organisational deficiencies are aggravated by an acute shortage of qualified planners and policy-makers, which often results in the placing of unqualified people in positions of great responsibility. This is especially true at the local level, but in varying degrees it permeates all levels of government. The problems that confront policy-makers trying to operate effectively in this sort of situation are made worse by an acute shortage of relevant information on which to base policies. Sufficiently detailed statistics relating to the various policy sectors are difficult and costly to assemble.

In these circumstances the goals and objectives established by planners and policy-makers are often incomplete and contain unresolved conflicts. Policy goals are established for specific sectors of national life, particularly those concerned with economic changes, which either do not take account of social and environmental factors or conflict with other goals established within government departments concerned with social and environmental management. In addition, specific goals and objectives are often unrealistic in that they seek more than can be achieved even with the most extraordinary use of available resources. Often they do not specify the steps to be taken to achieve the desired end. Moreover, the strategy adopted often ignores the evolutionary and gradual nature of the process at work and requires radical changes in the existing momentum of development which cannot be attained.

At the regional level in most countries planning tends to be confined to physical aspects and is often informal and unofficial. Except in the case of national regions which are provinces or states with their own governments, regional planning is usually an *ad hoc* function directed by appointed officials with very limited powers to make decisions or to review the decisions of local authorities and central government agencies which affect the region. The task is often given to a committee of regional directors of national agencies, and in such circumstances it is the more powerful and larger agencies — such as transportation — that dominate the group and make it impossible to achieve the integration of sectoral programmes.

At the local level planning has long been a function of many municipal authorities. Being directly linked to the problems and expectations of the people, local planning departments have been relatively more responsive to their needs. Moreover, the architects and physical planners who have dominated planning at local level detected quite early most of the physical environmental problems. However, local planning has been severely limited by a number of factors. Firstly, lacking precise analytical tools to understand economic and social forces, it has been unable to predict accurately the environmental changes brought about by such forces. Secondly, since central governments generally have not recognised that urban growth and development are national issues, the burden of improvement has fallen on local authorities using their own resources even though they lack the instruments for controlling growth. Thirdly, most municipal boundaries predate the present scale of urban areas. Cities have spread beyond their original boundaries, presenting rural authorities with problems which are outside the scope of their experience and resources. Fourthly, many local authorities have only limited functions; other local functions within their areas are discharged by central government departments and agencies or by public bodies, neither of which are answerable to the local authority for their actions.

This combination of functional and territorial fragmentation has frustrated urban decision-making and action and has brought delays and conflicts. The autonomy of sectoral agencies has resulted in unco-ordinated decisions, omissions and costly errors. Because of organisational problems, policies and plans are frequently ill-conceived and poorly co-ordinated both functionally and territorially. In many cases they are also undermined by insufficient popular support due to a lack of public participation in the decision-making process. The result of all these managerial and organisational inadequacies has been a rapid deterioration of the urban environment, reflected in overcrowded and insanitary living conditions, lack of services, badly related land uses, a heavy dependence on motor transport and (in developing countries particularly) large squatter settlements without even the most elementary facilities.

Comprehensive planning is the means of bringing together for a common purpose the policies, plans and programmes carried out in the various sectors and at the various levels of government. The nature and degree of comprehensive planning varies widely between the nations which have adopted such a system. It is most highly developed in countries with centrally planned economies such as the U.S.S.R., Poland, Czechoslovakia, Rumania and Hungary, but examples can also be found in Sweden, France, the Netherlands, Turkey, Israel, Ghana and Pakistan.

A fully developed comprehensive planning system should involve the integration of economic, social and physical planning at the national level to provide a policy framework for similarly integrated planning at regional and local levels. The process should involve:

1. Guidance and participation in the formulation of goals at policy-making levels.

2. Assembling and maintaining a data base adequate for the decisions and changes that are to be considered.

3. A process of systematic evaluation of alternative policies, objectives and projects.

4. Anticipation of the results of trends and technological changes and consideration of both the long-term and short-term implications of decisions.

5. Acceptance of the need to bring about changes by positive actions and to distribute equitably the benefits and costs of change.

6. Willingness to work out possible solutions and preferred courses of action with all the parties concerned.

Problems of Methodology

The above discussion indicates that comprehensive planning should be seen as a necessary tool for improving the environment of settlements but a number of problems inhibit its optimum application. Since various forms of comprehensive planning are used in various countries the relevance of the following comments to different national situations depends upon prevailing social, economic and cultural institutions and on the nature of the planning activity.

One of the most difficult problems in the comprehensive planning process is the clarification of ends and means and of the relationship between them. Often goals are established without full knowledge of the means for their achievement, in which case it is most unlikely that they will be achieved. Often, too, conflicts among goals are unresolved. A related tendency is to try to separate ends and means artificially: they are part of a single analytical continuum and must be treated as such. Goals should be stated in such a way that progress towards them can be measured; only then do they provide meaningful criteria for evaluating plans. Comprehensive plans by their nature seek the achievement of many goals affecting many sectors. When, as often happens, the people affected are not involved in the selection of goals, it becomes difficult to obtain their commitment to the plan. Here again the chance of achieving the goals is impaired. The problems of methodology involved in formulating goals and their relationship to other components of the planning process must be resolved before a framework can be established for subsequent steps. Procedures must be developed by which goals can be related to specific objectives and by which sets of goals can be made consistent as between national, regional and local levels.

Once goals are specified the next difficulty is encountered in the identification of actions which will achieve the stated objectives. This requires an understanding of the basic forces and relationships shaping the development of settlements. There are at least two critical dimensions to this issue — the quality of the information and the way it is used to predict the consequences of alternative courses of action. Simulation of complex systems of settlements involves working with a broad range of qualitative and quantitative variables, not all of which can be expressed in terms of technical data. Often a problem is not defined comprehensively because the definition is done by one professional discipline or one government

department using the narrow analytical tools with which it is
familiar. If the problem is not comprehensively defined the
plan which emerges cannot take account of the full range of
consequences.

The use of mathematical models has been helpful in
explaining some urban phenomena but those developed so far
are not sophisticated enough to provide guidance for influ-
encing trends of urban growth and change. Much remains to
be learned about the phenomena of urban development.
More precise indicators are needed with which to measure
change and to evaluate it. The broader use of comprehensive
planning will be greatly stimulated by the construction of a
substantive urban development theory which will facilitate
evaluation of the consequences of development decisions.

Many new methods are being evolved to improve the
planning process. Techniques such as planning-programming-
budgeting are being used to link long-term and short-term
plans. Efforts are being made in the preparation of plans to
specify the political, economic and administrative steps
necessary for their implementation. Planners are learning the
value of evaluating past planning efforts and there is a greater
willingness to experiment and monitor the results.

To be effective, however, comprehensive planning must be
used at all levels of government, and this introduces some
additional problems. To what degree should the process be
centralised or decentralised? How are local and regional
considerations to be built into national plans, and vice versa?
Mechanisms are needed to sort out the scope and impact of
plans at various levels so that the interests of those involved
can be properly considered. It is also essential to have
efficient channels of communication between the three
levels. Information must flow freely for a system to function
effectively.

It should be the specific responsibility of some government
unit to design the comprehensive planning system and its
essential linkages and communication channels with other
departments, agencies and levels of government, and to
monitor its operation to ensure that it works efficiently and
effectively across all sectors and through all levels. The
system should be subjected to cost-effectiveness studies.

Criteria should be established to guide the allocation of effort within the planning process so that the results are timely and justify what is spent on them.

Comprehensive planning at the national level attempts to control and direct the activities of various government departments through a central planning agency. Unless effective links are established to ensure that co-ordination does take place the attempt cannot succeed. And since other government agencies will implement the plan it is important to establish close working relations among all the agencies concerned. It is particularly important that the people who will carry out the plan are involved in the plan-making process, so that they become committed to its implementation. Good inter-agency information systems are essential to ensure that the executive departments act within the comprehensive planning framework continuously rather than on a project-by-project basis. It is vital that the national budgeting process should be related constantly to the comprehensive planning process.

Even where organisational changes are made they cannot and do not ensure that the constraints of professional training, skills and interests are overcome. Problems of internal communication within an organisation or department can be just as difficult as problems of communication between organisations. What matters in the short term is the development of understanding between different spheres of expertise; and in the long run, perhaps, the growth of new, differently aligned spheres of expertise. A continuous debate is needed within professional groups, between professional groups (which must recognise that their boundaries are constantly changing), between experts and politicians, neither of whom can be effective without the other, and between planners and the planned, since planning is essentially a political process in which public awareness, support and participation are crucial. For the expert the biggest difficulty perhaps lies in appreciating the contribution that can be made by other experts – especially by politicians, whose expertise lies in deciding what action is desirable, appropriate and acceptable to the people they represent. The most important issues can be decided only in political terms.

Traditional areas of academic study and in-service training need to be integrated to produce the new breed of multi-disciplinary planners suited to the comprehensive approach. In addition to the traditional land-use planning techniques, planners need to acquire knowledge and skills in some at least of the following fields: information processing, operations research, policy analysis, decision theory, probability theory, statistics, systems management, geography, social and political science and economics. However, it will remain necessary, in dealing with the more complex planning problems, to employ teams of specialists in the various related disciplines.

The Administrative System

An administrative structure responsible for producing policies and plans will need some or all of the following features: an agency charged with evaluating and redesigning the policy-making structure and process; an agency specifically responsible for long-range policy-making and for keeping abreast of new knowledge and research; strong links between the units involved in policy-making and execution; a significant opportunity for individuals, interest groups and other organisations to contribute to the policy-making process.

Since environmental problems result from or affect so many aspects of government policy they can be dealt with successfully only by a comprehensive approach. This is not possible within the traditional compartmentalised system of government. Fundamental reforms of the system are needed to make it possible to formulate environmental policies, to ensure that environmental factors are given proper weight in decision-making, and to unify responsibility for monitoring environmental development and achieving improvements. In most countries it may be necessary to centralise in one agency the responsibility for monitoring environmental conditions, developing policies and programmes and enforcing controls. The process of reform may, perhaps, not be completed until there is a new generation of public officials able and willing to temper their sectoral interests with concern for environmental quality.

Government agencies and the public sector should be

required to take account of the environmental side-effects of their development activities — such as the building of roads, power stations and industrial plants — as well as of their economic desirability and engineering feasibility. In planning such schemes an inter-disciplinary approach is needed to ensure the integrated use of the physical and social sciences and the art of environmental design. Evaluation of a development project should include an analysis of its probable direct and indirect impact on the environment, including its effect on such factors as population distribution, water purity and public utilities. It should always be borne in mind that while projects may have a small impact individually their cumulative effect may be significant. Where work on the project has already begun, means should be found to minimise adverse environmental consequences by subsequent action. Time should always be allowed for public examination and comment on projects before action is taken to implement them.

In any hierarchical structure of administration there is always a dilemma whether to emphasise sectoral or areal coherence in decision-taking. If the stress is placed on integrating all decisions relating to a particular sector there is a tendency to strong vertical subordination of lower to higher levels of administration. This is a prominent feature of most government systems particularly in developing countries. It produces a strong hierarchy of central government departments with field administrations of limited authority. The line of decision-making is long and the process slow. The resulting structural separation of local units hinders the co-ordination of decision-making in the different sectors within an area. Such co-ordination often has to take place at the national level, gravely impeding coherence at the lower level.

These disadvantages are being increasingly recognised. Many countries are making efforts to strengthen arrangements at the regional level for the integration of planning, decision-making and administration. This has led to the creation of multi-purpose regional units bringing together the regional offices of central departments or the elected local authorities or a mixture of the two. This arrangement allows the exercise of greater discretion at the regional level; at the same time regional co-ordination of sectoral policies is strengthened and decision-making is accelerated.

This emphasis on regional integration should not allow vertical co-ordination to be neglected, but policies and decisions taken at the higher level should provide only a general framework within which more detailed decisions can be taken at the lower level. Such a division of responsibility is a prerequisite for the co-ordination of decision-making and action by authorities at different levels.

The boundaries of regional and local units of government which are to be responsible for comprehensive planning and the co-ordinated administration of sectoral policies should be defined, not by reference to existing territorial divisions, but on the basis of present-day social and economic relationships and of the appropriate catchment areas for the functions exercised by the authority. The structure of local administration in many countries is still tied to the geography of an agrarian culture in which land was the main source of production and government functions were minimal. But modern urban man no longer finds his food, shelter and security within a limited geographical habitat. The individual and collective needs of people who are concentrated in settlements are met from a variety of often distant sources. In designing a system of comprehensive planning and administration, governments must develop the high degree of network co-ordination that characterises modern business and industry when its interests cross historical boundaries.

Lower-level authorities should have a fair amount of discretion in the decisions they take, even in respect of how they should implement the decisions of higher-level authorities. But there must be good channels of communication between levels. Information about the region should flow upwards as an input to national planning and decision-making while the framework and guidelines provided by high-level policies and decisions should be clearly communicated to the low-level authorities. A greater degree of discretion for lower-level authorities is already apparent in many countries, including some of those with highly centralised governmental systems — a striking example being Yugoslavia. A number of developing countries have recently introduced a system of regional administration providing some degree of decentralisation or delegation of decision-making. In several European countries proposals have been made to increase the size of local authorities to make them viable and effective units for planning and other functions, thus lessening their dependence on central government.

The establishment at regional level of an agency entrusted with comprehensive planning and the administration of a number of major functions strengthens the case for a democratically elected regional authority. This is because policy co-ordination at the regional level implies that policy decisions should be taken at that level and such decisions are a matter for politicians rather than officials. A comprehensive regional administration cannot function dynamically if the ties of its various departments to central government ministries remain strong, for this retards and stultifies proper co-ordination at the regional level.

It is becoming increasingly necessary at the regional and local levels to provide for greater public participation in the decision-making process. Apparently arbitrary and bureaucratic actions by governments in respect of highway routes, housing and urban renewal projects, schools and other public facilities have often resulted in harmful rather than beneficial effects on some sectors of the population. Neighbourhoods have been divided or cut off from essential facilities as the result of such decisions. Often the authorities have not given enough thought to the social and economic impact of projects on families and businesses which have been obliged to move. Errors of judgement such as these have alerted citizens to the widespread and vital effects of government actions and have led them to organise in opposition to decisions in which they have not participated or even been kept fully informed. Provision for maximum local participation in decisions affecting an area is therefore becoming standard practice in many countries.

To sum up, the adoption of a comprehensive approach to the environment of settlements is likely to involve a complete overhaul of the structure of government. Specifically, it requires the creation at national, regional and local levels of

machinery to formulate environmental policies and to prepare and implement plans and programmes of environmental
development as an integrated part of economic and social
development plans and programmes. This will involve creating or strengthening regional and local authorities; revising
their functions in accordance with present needs and simplifying their relations with national authorities; establishing a
hierarchy of planning and decision-making agencies at national, regional and local levels with provision for inter-
communication, integration of policies, plans and actions and
maximum public participation; and instituting a process of
reviewing the environmental implications of all decisions and
projects at each level.

Such machinery is necessary to respond to contemporary
problems of technological and social change and to assure
firm progress in economic development with safeguards for
the environment. Highest priority should be given to national
intersectoral planning and to reviewing the environmental
implications of all decisions. Development of a system of
national, regional and local planning and decision-making
should proceed as rapidly as resources permit. In developing
countries such a reform will take time, but these countries
can establish immediately a process of reviewing all decisions
in the light of their environmental implications. The cost of
improved decision-making machinery is minimal and should
be greatly outweighed by the savings which result from
avoiding bad decisions.

Legal, Fiscal and Institutional Machinery
The adoption of comprehensive planning involves the creation not only of an appropriate government structure and
procedures but also of appropriate legal, fiscal and institutional machinery to help to carry out development programmes in a harmonious and efficient manner.

In many countries the laws relating to planning and
development are inadequate. Often there is no law establishing and defining the planning function in government, or if
one exists its provisions are not appropriate to present needs.
In consequence, development is haphazard, with improper
mixtures of land uses and congestion due to excessive

densities; uncontrolled speculation causes land costs to rise beyond feasible limits for housing and public use; and residential areas are developed which are not related to other elements of the urban system and lack public utilities and services.

An appropriate legal system should include laws establishing the planning function in government and providing for the control and direction of development, and codes regulating land use, building standards, sanitary arrangements and property maintenance. To be effective such laws and codes should be not only adequate in their provisions but also properly enforced. Legal systems must be interrelated with other government programmes and institutions affecting the development and management process. For example, tax systems conceived solely on the basis of tax criteria, such as yield and ease of collection, may conflict with land-planning policies. Where the aims of these two systems are not co-ordinated, neither is well served. These interrelationships are intricate and are generally not apparent without careful analysis. The analysis should begin with policies and trace the effects of laws to determine whether they help or obstruct the implementation of the policies. These interrelationships differ between nations, reflecting differences in administrative, economic and legal systems, and need therefore to be analysed separately for each country.

Planning legislation should establish a national planning agency charged with preparing and updating a national development plan and with reviewing development decisions and projects. It may also establish a national planning board or committee composed, at least in part, of the heads of relevant ministries such as industry, housing, transport, public works, social welfare, local government and natural resources.

Legislation should also establish regional and local planning bodies and prescribe their duties and responsibilities. It should give planning authorities the power to require that all development complies with officially adopted plans; this responsibility is usually placed at the local level, with provision for review at higher levels. It should give the authorities the power of compulsory land acquisition to carry out development schemes. Some planning laws allow land to be reserved for future public use for roads, community facilities, and so on, with provision for compensation only when the land is actually acquired. Planning authorities are usually empowered to adopt land-use controls or bylaws covering the purpose, density and design of private developments.

An associated system of codes regulating the use and operation of buildings and land may include sanitary codes covering water supply and sewage disposal systems and the disposal of solid wastes; construction codes governing the safety of buildings and building components; housing codes setting out space, light and ventilation requirements; codes covering drainage, flood control and land excavation and fill, and air and water pollution and noise prevention codes.

The complexity and breadth of planning acts vary with the size and resources of the country, its stage of development, type of economy and the scale and nature of its environmental problems. In developing countries the planning machinery and its supporting legislation can be enacted in stages, but as a minimum local development controls and the power to review projects in the light of their environmental implications should be instituted.

National economic and fiscal systems have generally evolved independently of legal systems and policies governing land development and environmental protection, with the result that these systems are usually insufficiently related to one another and often in conflict. In many cases public accounting and tax systems encourage and subsidise poor development and environmental degradation. They evaluate the costs and benefits of development projects in purely economic terms, ignoring or giving inadequate regard to social and environmental costs. Tax systems often encourage land speculation and poor building practices. In most countries transportation programmes are consciously designed to provide substantial subsidies to the private motorist while public transport systems are allowed to deteriorate or, if non-existent, are not encouraged to develop. This results firstly in a large allocation of public funds (which never seem to catch up with the needs) to roads and parking; and secondly in increasingly serious problems of air pollution from vehicle exhausts and congestion on urban roads.

Methods of national income accounting should be developed which more fully reflect the true social and environmental costs of development decisions. For example, new industrial plants will on the benefit side increase employment and income, but if the plant is badly located in relation to the homes of its workers or the services it needs, or sited without full consideration of its impact on the environment, additional costs may be incurred. Similar problems can be created in the development of transport facilities and in commercial and residential development. More complete methods of cost-benefit analysis which take into account the indirect costs of social and environmental factors should, therefore, be applied to investment decisions. Although in many cases only rough approximations of such indirect costs can be quantified, even these can throw new light on decisions.

Pricing mechanisms, subsidies, tax penalties and incentives and similar devices can be used to correct management practices which have adverse social and environmental effects, or to bring about development which is more in accord with public policies. These measures may include requiring those who pollute the environment to pay part or all of the cost of correcting the damage. They may also support planning controls by deterring land uses in locations where they will create adverse environmental effects or by encouraging them where they will be less damaging or will have socially or environmentally beneficial effects. They can also be used to encourage development of better quality.

Urban development policies and programmes need the support of urban land reform, particularly in developing countries. Urban land should be regarded as a public resource, to be husbanded and conserved like water, minerals and agriculturally productive land. Governments should therefore assume responsibility for manipulating land market mechanisms and making land available for use, and for the financing — or arranging the financing — of urban land-development programmes. They should perform a major role as land developers in urban areas, by providing infrastructure, housing and services and by participating in joint ventures with the private sector in housing, commerce and industry.

Speculation in urban land should be strictly controlled or eliminated as a danger to the well-being of society and a threat to the achievement of economic and social objectives. Reserve land for future urban expansion should be acquired for development in accordance with local and regional land-use plans. The price of land, whether sold voluntarily or acquired by compulsory purchase, should be fixed by the assessed tax valuation of the property in order to hinder speculation and increase the income derived from the real property tax. The principle of expropriating under-used land, which is found in modern agrarian legislation, should be applied in urban areas to land that owners are withholding from the market for speculative purposes. The increased value of private land resulting from public works should be taxed to return at least part of the benefit to the public. Strong systems should be established to control the cost of land intended for housing, since speculation in available land complicates and undermines efforts to deal with the problem of housing low-income groups. New towns should be developed with public funds so as to provide housing and employment opportunities that are an attractive alternative to unplanned settlements around overburdened urban centres. In developing countries where migrants to urban areas are creating transitional settlements, governments should give priority to meeting their urgent housing needs by financing the preparation of land and installing essential public utilities and services.

The forging of effective agencies and institutions to implement development policies is as important as the formulation of the policies and plans themselves. Agencies must be properly organised, adequately financed and staffed with trained personnel under aggressive and efficient leadership. It takes time to build up effective agencies, to create close working relationships between them and other public and private bodies and to gain the confidence and respect of the individuals and agencies with which they must collaborate.

Agencies may be needed in the following sectors: land

purchase and assembly, infrastructure financing and construction; transportation; housing finance and construction; housing management and the rehousing of people displaced by public projects; code enforcement; public facilities and services; planning control of private development; open space, recreation and tourism; resource management; preservation of monuments. In developing countries and in small countries several of these functions may be combined in one agency, at least until the responsibilities grow large enough to justify their separation.

Problems in Developing Countries

The developing countries face a different set of problems from those of the more developed countries in creating an environmental planning system. In the first place the nature and causes of their environmental problems are very different. By and large they do not have to cope with the massive pollution of the environment by industrial and consumer wastes which characterises the affluent societies of the developed world. On the contrary they are in a position to see that these unpleasant and destructive side-effects of economic growth are avoided, or at least kept to a minimum, in their own economic development. Their main environmental problems arise from poverty and the lack of basic amenities such as decent houses, water supply and sanitary arrangements, especially in rural areas and urban transitional settlements.

A second important difference lies in their shortage of resources to meet these problems. This means that they must adopt a gradual and progressive approach which places emphasis on helping and encouraging people to improve their own living conditions and surroundings. An essential first step in this direction is to create public awareness and understanding of the importance of environmental issues and to modify the prevalent belief that economic growth is beneficial regardless of its environmental consequences.

The highly centralised structure of government and the shortage of trained manpower in most developing countries means that the first moves to establish a comprehensive planning and management system must be simple and feasible. It is vitally important to make the best use of scarce manpower resources and the organisations that are available. Rational policy formulation and comprehensive planning take time to achieve; in the meantime steps can be taken to evaluate the social and environmental implications of development projects before they are carried out, to monitor the performance of existing industrial plants and to enforce anti-pollution regulations.

Immediate action should also be possible to conserve natural resources and to protect natural and man-made features of historic, scientific and aesthetic value. It may not be possible immediately to acquire land and carry out restoration and reclamation work in pursuit of such policies, but it should be possible at least to designate sites to prevent their destruction or degradation by other activities.

Most countries should be able at least to make a start on reforming legal and fiscal systems and establishing necessary agencies, particularly if international aid programmes are expanded to meet the growing need. With technical assistance and broader programmes for the training of professional personnel, rapid progress can be made towards the development of at least the organisational framework for improved environmental management. The help of international agencies in creating a climate of understanding and concern and in assisting poorer countries to develop the management approaches and tools necessary for environmental protection and enhancement is perhaps the most urgent task on the international agenda in this decade.

Public Support

Action to reduce, solve or forestall environmental problems begins with the recognition that such problems exist and that many of them are serious threats to human welfare and even to the survival of human society. Although there is probably no country in the world today where there is not at least some concern about environmental problems, the degree of recognition and concern varies widely. Among many national and, even more, local political leaders there is indifference, disbelief and resistance to calls for action to protect and enhance the environment. In consequence people's opportunities are narrowed and they are subjected to unnecessary inconvenience and expense by decisions which, though not directly concerned with the environment, have a pronounced impact upon it.

The adoption of comprehensive planning for environmental improvement calls for changes in current attitudes, habits and values among politicians, officials, organisations and individuals, and for changes too in some of the fundamental structures, life-styles and institutions which have enabled peoples and nations to survive, and some of them to prosper. Such changes cannot be easily or quickly achieved. The forces that have conspired to produce our current development trajectories have considerable momentum and will not be easily deflected. Many people will find it difficult to accept the idea that the past is no longer the guide to the future. More will find it difficult to accept the postponement of present gratification for future improvement — for this is what comprehensive environmental planning implies. Only by extensive education in environmental values (which ought to begin in school) can people be brought to accept willingly the need to make sacrifices.

In the past most people have become concerned about the environment in which they live only when it has directly touched some aspect of their personal lives. Only very recently have people begun to become involved in the shaping of their surroundings by participation in the planning process. What we need now, if progress is to be made, is a general refusal to accept environmental degradation passively. Such an attitude must depend upon a popular understanding of the nature of settlements, how they may be shaped, and how this is a continuing process that can make possible an enriched life. Individual citizens conscious of their environmental rights will be the strongest insurance that future generations will enjoy the best possible environment. Through comprehensive planning they will be able to guide and direct the use of technology rather than allow technology's own momentum to dictate the way they live their lives.

A programme of environmental improvement cannot rest on government action alone: it must also enlist the active support of industry, commerce and agriculture, trade unions

and professional associations, the universities, scientific societies and civic action groups. Public participation in plan-
making and voluntary compliance with plans is one of the
most effective and economical means of ensuring that
policies are implemented.

Research, Education and Training
Comprehensive environmental planning and management is a
relatively new field which has not yet been subjected to
intensive research and development programmes. The research that has taken place in recent years has been largely
confined to a relatively small number of highly urbanised
countries and has dealt very little with the problems of
developing countries. Professional training for planners and
other specialists in settlement development and environmental fields has also been concentrated in these same
countries, with the exception of a few new institutions in
developing countries.

The United Nations and its agencies have provided the
main leadership in the development of knowledge and
training in the developing world. In the United Nations
system the unit primarily concerned with the development of
human settlement is the Centre for Housing, Building and
Planning. Other significant programmes affecting aspects of
settlement development are operated by the World Health
Organisation (WHO), the Food and Agriculture Organisation
(FAO), the International Labour Organisation (ILO), the
United Nations Educational, Scientific and Cultural Organisation (UNESCO) and the United Nations Industrial Development Organisation (UNIDO). The United Nations regional
economic commissions are also playing an increasingly
important role. Technical assistance projects financed by the
United Nations Development Programme, as well as those
financed by individual nations, have produced a number of
significant results. More recently the large international
investment organisations such as the International Bank for
Reconstruction and Development and the Inter-American
Development Bank have indicated an interest in a broader
approach to investment projects, including greater consideration of the impact of projects on the total sphere of human

settlements, using comprehensive planning as a tool for project evaluation.

Although significant progress has been made in recent years in the expansion of knowledge of settlement planning and development, and its application through technical assistance and training programmes, the scope and level of these efforts is insufficient to cope with the growing magnitude of the problem, particularly in the developing world. A greater effort is needed at both national and international levels. At the nation level, institutes of settlement development should be established to become the focal point of such activity. These might be operated by a government agency but should preferably be attached to a university as an adjunct to a department of environmental studies.

The activities needed can be grouped under the three main headings of Monitoring, Research and Dissemination. Monitoring activities should include the gathering of qualitative and quantitative data on changes taking place in settlements, including population growth, urbanisation, industrialisation, housing, transitional settlements and air, water and noise pollution. Research activities should include analysis of demographic and environmental changes and the formulation of theories, policies and methods for improving the development of settlements. The areas for research might include policy formation processes, comprehensive planning techniques and processes, government and administrative organisation, legal systems, economic and fiscal measures and the forms and functions of agencies for implementing policies, plans and programmes. Dissemination activities at the national level should focus on professional training and public education.

In developing countries, where shortage of professional personnel is greatest, the urgent need should be met by training at secondary school and undergraduate university level. Longer-term needs require the creation of faculties of environmental planning at universities to provide inter-disciplinary programmes for the training of professional planners. Smaller nations could best establish such courses at a regional university serving a group of countries, so that the wide interdisciplinary range needed could be met. In developed countries additional post-graduate courses in comprehensive planning with a greater interdisciplinary scope should be provided. This scope should include, in addition to physical planning, courses in the social sciences and specialised fields such as statistics and information processing, operations research, systems analysis and management.

To educate the general public on environmental issues and the citizen's role in environmental improvement, these subjects should be incorporated in primary and secondary school curricula. The press, radio, television, films and exhibitions should be used to take the message to the general public. Public participation in planning and decision-making is itself an educative process.

It is recognised that in most developing countries it will be possible in the short term only to institute some basic monitoring activities and to undertake training to sub-professional standards. All other activities will have to be organised on a multi-national basis under the aegis of the United Nations and its affiliates and regional economic commissions.

Comprehensive planning is a relatively new tool and its techniques still need developing and refining. Specifically, there are four broad areas where expansion and improvement are clearly needed: monitoring of urban and environmental phenomena; research in planning theory and its analytical techniques; communications systems for exchanging and disseminating information, and co-ordinating machinery for bridging organisational gaps in the horizontal and vertical planes.

It is quite evident that much of the information we have been collecting about settlements is either inaccurate or irrelevant. But unless we know what state we are in today and are alerted to changes as they take place our ability to plan deliberately is seriously impaired. Settlement planning needs the sort of indicators of change that economists have long used to monitor changes in the national economy and to design adjustments to economic policies and programmes. It is vital, therefore, that we should develop appropriate data systems so that we can measure changes in the environment as they occur and take preventative action before crisis situations are reached. The systems need to be co-ordinated at all levels so that the national picture can be both built up from local information and broken down and separated into component parts. In this way local and regional effects of national programmes can be measured and the total national effect of all programmes can be assessed. Information collected at national, regional and local levels will make it easier to compare different parts of a country; if the information systems are designed on an international basis they will also help the exchange of information between countries.

Research into planning theory and methodology is directly related to monitoring activities because it is through research that the relevant questions that need to be asked are formulated. Our present knowledge about the cause-and-effect relationships within settlements is too limited for the objectives we wish to achieve. The problem confronting comprehensive planning is the analysis and integration of a vast number of interdependent variables, the structural relationships of which must be understood before the directions of change can be established. Managing and analysing such complex systems require higher levels of abstraction than those currently being used. Simulation models and other mathematical structures will have to be developed, involving extensive use of computers, if we are to understand the settlement system. The assumptions and inputs that go into such planning models will vary considerably between nations because of differences in social, political and economic traditions and circumstances. Each nation therefore needs its own research programme.

The better dissemination of information can be achieved by a number of means, including exchange visits, educational programmes and demonstration projects. It is important to note that control over information carries with it an element of political power and is often used to perpetuate the autonomy of government departments. Since comprehensive planning needs inputs from diverse sources, social and political obstacles impeding the flow of information must be removed. Failure to provide good and clear channels of communication produces duplication of effort by various departments and the formulation of proposals in isolation and without sufficient knowledge. Neither of these conditions can be tolerated if comprehensive planning is to function effectively.

Even within a comprehensive planning framework a high degree of discretion may be left to various departments charged with implementing various aspects of the plan. In such a situation administrators in a particular agency may be required to make a whole series of decisions that were not explicitly covered in the plan. It is vital, therefore, to have machinery by which such decisions can be tested and co-ordinated with other elements in the plan. Devices to co-ordinate continuously the activities of various departments are absolutely essential to comprehensive planning.

Data collection and research can be costly activities especially if they are not co-ordinated and carefully programmed. It is therefore important that monitoring activities should be staged so that the outputs appear at the right time and can be used effectively in the planning process. Similarly the research agenda should be aligned to the nation's development priorities and problems so that the studies undertaken have a good chance of making a direct contribution to the development process. If monitoring and research are geared to the nation's needs and are directed at high priority problems, the cost will be more than offset by the savings which come from better decisions.

Part Two

5 Housing

The Residential Environment

No part of man's environment affects his health and
well-being more directly than the house in which he seeks
shelter, security, comfort and dignity. The home environment helps to shape his life and attitudes; it creates the
setting in which he begins and ends his days, in which he is
educated, marries, raises children and associates with his
fellow men. The home represents what a man believes in,
what he will protect. It influences his sense of civic and
communal responsibility and relates him to his physical
surroundings and to the history and culture of his community.

It is now generally recognised that many of these
attributes of the individual house hold true also for the wider
setting in which the house is placed: the neighbourhood or
residential district. Thus, when designing and planning houses
we have come to think not just of the individual dwelling but
also of the juxtaposition of many houses, and of the services,
facilities and structures which support and complement the
individual house and make up the residential environment.

This chapter examines some of the qualities of design,
construction, provision and layout which seem essential in
the residential environment if it is to contribute fully to
human health and happiness. But it should be clear from the
outset that these are guidelines and targets rather than rigid
specifications. A set of specific standards and criteria may
not always be applicable within a single country, let alone
throughout the international community. The housing and
environmental problems of transitional urban areas and rural
settlements in developing countries, for example, could never
be solved by attempts to replace them with dwellings and
neighbourhoods conforming to the highest desirable standards. The problem is too big and the resources are too small
for that sort of approach. Even in the advanced industrialised

101

countries the number of new houses built each year does not exceed three per cent of the existing stock. Priority must, therefore, be given to improving inadequate existing facilities and providing basic utilities and services where none exist, for excessive demand on water supplies, toilets and so on lies at the very root of some of the social problems of housing.

It is clear also that the establishment of standards based on a preconceived relationship between people's social well-being and the physical environment is no longer valid. Such relationships must be critically examined and their scientific basis explored and tested. The standards which emanate from a social concept of housing must be rooted in the broadest interpretation of individual and societal needs.

The establishment of national standards for housing and the residential environment should fall into two parts: firstly, the assessment of the special housing and community-service needs of the aged, of the young and of low-income or otherwise disadvantaged groups, and, secondly, the creation of an integrated system of standards covering all the elements in the residential environment. The first is a step towards the second. Solutions cannot, of course, wait on the establishment of acceptable standards. Action should be taken to deal with housing problems even though knowledge of how they should be comprehensively tackled is not complete.

Governments should, however, seek to establish obligatory minimum standards, together with the dates by which it is hoped to see them attained. To be realistic, such standards must be based on an appraisal of the resources available for meeting them, of social and cultural characteristics in the country, region or locality concerned, and of the existing housing and urban development situation. They should be accompanied by machinery for monitoring progress and for enforcing compliance with the standards. For economic or technical reasons it may be wise to adopt working standards that are lower than the target minimum standard, but a check should be kept on how rapidly the gap between the two is being closed. Building codes and regulations can be designed to achieve better housing at lower resource cost and to encourage the development of building technologies appropriate to locally available materials.

Progress towards the adoption of more precise intersectoral standards for housing and community facilities must depend on the collection of new data and the analysis of existing data by new methods. It may be useful to set up at the highest level in the planning system an interdisciplinary and intersectoral group of experts to review and analyse existing information and standards and perhaps to recommend alternative standards for housing and community facilities along the lines suggested in this chapter.[1]

The House and the Neighbourhood

Housing and the residential environment should provide shelter from the weather, including extremes of weather; freedom from sources and carriers of disease; security from dangers and nuisances; adequate space for sleeping, preparing and eating food, storage, individual and family privacy, recreation and social and cultural activities; access to places of work, shops and community services; and opportunities for commercial and communal development.

In physical terms, houses should be weatherproof, keeping out the wind and the rain and maintaining a comfortable indoor temperature and atmosphere. In some areas the structure may have to be designed to withstand earthquakes, floods, hurricanes or excessively heavy rain or snowfall. But everywhere careful attention should be paid to the juxtaposition of buildings and to their external surfaces, since these factors influence the buildings' capacity to retain or repel heat.[2] Many communities in hot, arid areas have a tradition of designing residential areas with narrow streets, white walls and shady courtyards which ameliorate the environment. Intelligent use of vegetation can also help in this respect.[3] Built-in controls of this kind are preferable to artificial air-conditioning plants, which are expensive in the energy they consume. In colder climates, district-heating schemes serving whole neighbourhoods may be more economical than individual heating units for each house and may have the added advantage of reducing air pollution.

Housing can be designed to ensure adequate ventilation, with particular care being exercised in the use of new building materials and techniques which may make the building virtually airtight. They should also be designed to admit as much sunlight or daylight as possible.

Houses should be reasonably free from disturbing outside noises and should provide reasonable sound insulation between rooms. A persistent problem in many countries is noise and vibration from airports, railways and main roads, which can seriously disturb household and community activities. Research studies suggest that low-frequency noises should not exceed thirty-five decibels in apartment houses.[4] The arrangement of buildings in relation to the source of a noise influences its transmission both outside and indoors. International attention should focus on the exchange of information in this area and on the development of comprehensive criteria for the control of noise transmission in the human environment.[5]

The amount of space required — or accepted — within the house will obviously vary with local customs and attitudes. Generally, people need a certain amount of privacy for sleeping, study and personal activities, and space for shared activities. There is no general agreement about the exact amount of space needed for various activities although there is some international acceptance of the view that houses with three or more people to each room are overcrowded. Overcrowding may create tensions and affect relationships both within the household and in the neighbourhood. This may be explained by the concept that each human activity has its own 'territory', and that when its boundaries are transgressed the individual responds in an undesirable or distorted way.

Housing should also provide links with the past. Wherever possible efforts should be made to preserve or restore well-built old houses. In several countries efforts have been made to preserve examples of building forms of different regions and periods; in some cases entire villages and communities have been preserved to maintain continuity with the past.

Every residential area needs a safe and adequate supply of water for drinking and domestic uses, for fire-fighting and for irrigation, and a safe system for removing and disposing of dirty water and human and household wastes. It has been internationally recommended that every house should have a water supply piped into the house or at least to a point within 100 metres of it; that every house should have a toilet and every urban house a flush toilet. In view of water shortages and the cost of sewage treatment and water purification it is questionable whether potable water should be used for cleaning and for disposing of wastes.

There should be regular and safe methods of removing household refuse which are consistent with healthy conditions in the neighbourhood and in the environment at large. The organisation of community refuse collection and disposal systems has become a question of major environmental concern in many cities. Present methods of removing excrement and refuse in the developed countries result in very high costs per household and steadily increasing pollution of the environment: they should not be adopted in developing countries, which could take advantage of this opportunity to learn from the mistakes of more advanced nations.

Another important environmental consideration is the planning and provision of neighbourhood roads and parking spaces. The need to accommodate an increasing number of vehicles often causes space originally meant for other purposes to be taken for parking. The necessary provision should be planned to minimise pollution and maximise the safety and comfort of pedestrians and residents. It can be much better accommodated on a community basis than within each building plot.

Many housing projects have failed to provide a satisfactory residential environment because they have been developed without proper regard to the co-ordinated provision of schools, shops, transport, meeting places and other essential supporting services and facilities. In addition to meeting individual needs, such amenities help to turn a collection of houses and families into a united community.

As progress is made in the mass-production of housing more attention will have to be paid to aesthetic considerations, relating the design of the development to the human scale and avoiding the visual monotony of excessive standardisation.

The neighbourhood, which is a vital cell in the network of human settlements, should be planned comprehensively whenever the opportunity presents itself, as it does in the development of new and expanding towns and in the redevelopment of old areas. Neighbourhood boundaries should not be too rigid, and space should be left within the neighbourhood for unknown future needs. The development of a workable neighbourhood plan calls for the active participation of the residents.

It is more appropriate to talk about criteria than about standards in relation to neighbourhood plans. Standards and criteria can be thought of as forming a continuum. Standards are measurable and should be capable of being legally enforced. Criteria are less measurable and cannot be legally enforceable: they provide only a basis for making judgements. A neighbourhood plan should state performance criteria based on broad aims such as the promotion of health, the enjoyment of a preferred life-style, the achievement of a high level of social well-being and the provision of adequate opportunities for self-fulfilment.

Locational Factors

A number of factors relating to both the natural and the man-made environment must be weighed in choosing the location of housing schemes. The micro-climate should be considered, and the nature of the terrain: does it have steep slopes or is it badly drained or subject to flooding or to seismic shocks? Some of these factors may preclude the use of the site for housing, while others may need to be taken into account in designing the layout of buildings and infrastructure. The location must also be considered in relation to other existing or intended elements in the urban structure — places of employment, shopping and service centres, transport systems, and the ease and economy with which the infrastructure can be extended to the new development. The timing of such extensions is important both for developing countries planning new residential areas and for developed countries, where too often whole blocks and neighbourhoods in central cities are demolished to await urban renewal which may only come years after an existing viable environment has been totally destroyed.

Housing areas should be conveniently close to areas of employment in terms of travel-to-work time — some countries try to limit this to about 10 per cent of a normal working day — but not so close that the residents will suffer pollution and other nuisances created by industrial processes. Too often the location of housing is decided only after the other major urban components, including industry, commerce, community facilities and transport systems, are established. This negates the aim of creating workable communities in which a healthy respect is shown for environmental considerations.

One key aim in the comprehensive planning of urban structures should be to relate housing and other elements to open space. It is possible to weave the natural environment into the urban structure in the form of large and small parks, playing-fields, footpaths, gardens and small patches of greenery, making up a network which extends through the urban area into the countryside beyond. Green open spaces help to keep the air clean and provide opportunities for healthy outdoor recreation. Often, in existing cities, the people who live furthest from recreational areas are those who cannot afford the transport to reach them — an unfortunate correlation of shortcomings in the physical and social structures. If properly related, all the elements of the urban structure can be composed into an organic unity. The aim should be to seek a proper development of the natural environment as well as its protection and conservation.

Social Involvement

Housing can contribute to the broader purposes of society as a whole as well as meeting the needs of the individual person and family. The physical arrangement of groups of houses, open spaces and meeting places in relation to other community institutions can enhance community awareness, promote civic responsibility and help to maintain a stable society. The ordered physical relationship of all types of housing to other components of the urban structure can help to ensure that no group is disadvantaged by reason of the sort of housing it occupies. Good housing can help to promote social integration if it is regarded as a basic human right to which all members of the community are entitled regardless of race, sex, religion or ethnic background. Moreover, an equal right of access to housing for all can help to ensure an equal right of access to other community facilities and services. This is particularly true in situations where access to other aspects of community life has historically been associated with a restricted right to housing.

The management of public housing can play an important part in community development: that is, 'the process by which efforts of people themselves are united with those of governmental authorities to improve the economic, social and cultural conditions of the community, to integrate these communities into the life of the nation and to enable them to contribute fully to national progress'.[6] The significant element here is the relationship between the housing authorities and tenants' associations, which should be seen in community development terms and not solely in terms of rent payments, problem families and unsatisfactory tenants.

Tenants' associations[7] on their own or in co-operation with housing management can be effective in inculcating good home management, in teaching the value of thrift and prudence in financial matters and in promoting civic responsibility. They can also act as channels for collecting and processing complaints. Their most important role may be that of providing an opportunity, through the education of tenants, to raise the general standard of living and to promote more effective action to improve the housing environment. The need for close co-operation between tenants' associations and public agencies cannot, therefore, be overemphasised. It is vital in this respect that there should be suitably trained people for the planning, organisation and management of housing.

Progressive Improvement in Transitional Areas

We stressed earlier that the standards and criteria discussed in this chapter may be seen by some countries as targets rather than norms, and that in certain circumstances any thought of attempting immediately to introduce high environmental standards would be out of the question. Nowhere is this more true than in the transitional settlements which form a large and growing part of many cities in the developing world.

Here the planning goal should be to identify, assist and underpin the forces of progressive improvement which the inhabitants of these areas often set in motion of their own accord.

Whether they are squatter settlements on vacant land or overcrowded central-area slums, transitional settlements play an important role in the urbanisation process in developing countries. A study of Calcutta[8] has identified six functions performed by the city's transitional settlements, known locally as 'bustee'.

(1) They provide housing at rents which are within the means of migrants; (2) they act as reception centres for migrants, helping them to adapt to urban life; (3) they provide within the bustee a wide variety of employment in marginal and small-scale enterprises; (4) they provide accommodation close to work; (5) their social and communal organisations provide essential social support in unemployment and other kinds of difficulty; (6) they encourage and reward small-scale private enterprise in the field of housing.

These six functions may be found in varying degrees in transitional settlements around the world, but their performance is inadequate and inefficient in relation to the level of need, primarily because of the lack of organised and systematic government help. The appalling conditions of environmental degradation found in transitional settlements both weaken the ability of the inhabitants to improve their surroundings and trigger government programmes that focus on the physical symptoms rather than the fundamental needs. Governments must identify and meet with selective investment those needs which the transitional groups cannot supply for themselves, thereby giving direct encouragement to the optimum use of popular resources in the process of progressive improvement.

Past experience indicates a number of critical areas in which governments can act to foster this process, including land tenure, employment, urban planning, community services, technical assistance and finance. There is clear evidence that the willingness of families in transitional areas to invest their own resources in improving their environment is directly dependent on their expectations of remaining on the land they occupy. Equally, their ability to improve their surroundings is directly and fundamentally related to the extent to which they can obtain adequate employment.

The physical capacity of a transitional area to sustain an improvement process depends on its location in relation to the urban area as a whole, its potential accessibility to the normal urban services such as water, sewers, electricity and transport, and the suitability of the site for residential use. The provision of health and education services, community development and other social support services affects both the willingness and the ability of the people to undertake improvements. Technical help is needed, particularly in the use of building materials and techniques, and its provision can directly improve the effectiveness with which popular resources are employed. There is evidence that the transitional groups can help to finance the improvement of their settlements by communal savings and credit schemes tied to housing and home improvement. Finally, it is evident that departmental specialisation in existing systems of government organisation commonly acts to block comprehensive programmes and that existing legislation may be inadequate to allow such programmes to be undertaken.

Unfortunately, not all transitional settlements are improving. Poor initial organisation, failure to plan for the linkage of the settlement with normal urban services and a mistaken choice of site may act singly or together to frustrate attempts at improvement and waste considerable popular resources. In such circumstances the community may reach a point where it can develop no further and will remain static or — which is more likely — will deteriorate and become a cancer on the city. Where the location or nature of the site rules out the provision of utilities and services, an alternative location for the settlement has to be found; but governments should try to keep such cases to a minimum by making creative attempts to link existing settlements to the urban system, for relocation projects can be costly both in their call on public funds and in the waste of popular resources they involve.

Central-city slums, which in some developing countries are generations or even centuries old, are not, for the most part, undergoing the kind of progressive improvement found in many squatter settlements. This may be due in large part to their being tenement areas where absentee landlords have no incentive to carry out improvements. It would be a mistake to see in this an indication that central slums should be considered separately from squatter and other uncontrolled settlements, for they usually play an important role in the transitional process. To the new migrants they offer some unique attractions, foremost among which are accommodation at rents they can afford and access to part-time jobs in the city centre. In effect they provide a reception centre for migrants.

Since the larger part of the population of these slums may be newcomers to urban life, and since long-established squatter settlements also tend to offer rented accommodation to newcomers, it is not normally possible to identify slum dwellers as essentially different from people in other transitional settlements. Rather, they should be seen as people at a different stage of transition. The task of the authorities is to find ways to eliminate the bad environmental conditions of these areas while strengthening their positive aspects. Incentives to environmental improvement have to be quite different from those designed for squatter settlements, with safeguards to ensure that slum landlords do not get an unearned windfall from measures to reduce residential densities and provide services.

To reduce overcrowding in slums the authorities should make available areas where people from the slums, and new arrivals who would otherwise swell the slum population, can settle. The emphasis here is on making available a site and basic facilities, not on providing housing. In present circumstances the construction of makeshift shelters on vacant land is often the only way large numbers of migrants can obtain a modicum of domestic security in the city. Squatting represents the most rational and positive response such people can make to their limited opportunities. But the settlements need not be unauthorised and uncontrolled. If the authorities provide the land in deliberately chosen localities and provide for the eventual extension of normal public utilities and services, the scene can be set for the controlled growth and progressive improvement of the settlement.

It is difficult to overstate the importance of achieving a major shift in attitude and emphasis away from the current norms of national and international policies and programmes for transitional areas and towards a new approach — one which accepts and supports their long-term existence and anticipates their future growth.

A Practical Approach

In conditions of rapid urban growth and even more rapid growth of transitional areas through migration and natural increase, vast clearance schemes with or without the provision of public housing can only aggravate the problems of people living in these areas. Such schemes can generally be regarded as destroying the human environment rather than improving it, as they commonly result in a reduction of the limited stock of housing within the economic reach of transitional groups, both by destroying the squatters' shacks and through a corresponding market pressure for increases in the rents of the remaining property. Public authorities at all levels should recognise that, in general, measures aimed at removing the transitional area population from the city will not succeed, and that developing economies cannot afford to build conventional public housing for these people.

The existence and needs of the areas concerned should be recognised, and their basic problems dealt with, initially at the national level. Legislation and administrative machinery should be developed which recognises the right to continued existence, and the need for improvement, of transitional areas. National policies should be formulated to provide a framework within which questions of land use, employment, urban planning, taxation and the provision of services can be dealt with at the local level. The objectives and actions of different levels of government and their sectoral agencies should be co-ordinated within a comprehensive planning framework which takes into account the relevant economic, social and physical aspects.

Government aid programmes could concentrate initially on improving the environmental context within which transitional-settlement housing is built, rather than on improving the individual houses, since it is the general setting which is the prime physical factor affecting the improvement potential of these areas. Specifically this means providing water supply and sewage disposal systems, electricity and community facilities and services. The legal and administrative system should be orientated to encourage popular efforts towards progressive improvement — for example, by revising the rigid building codes which cannot be met in transitional areas. These measures, in addition to helping to improve the environment, will also help the residents in their transition to full participation in urban life.

A fundamental implication of such actions is the recognition that the inhabitants of transitional areas are entitled to share the same healthy physical, social and economic environment as is enjoyed or aspired to by other urban dwellers. The cost of establishing a sound basis for short-term policies and programmes is minimal and can probably be met by reorientating existing programmes.

Governments and international organisations concerned with the environment of human settlements should now be ready to accept that urbanisation and the forces leading to the rapid growth of transitional settlements will continue to gain strength at least until the end of this century. This attitude should lead naturally towards planning in advance for the growth of transitional settlements in a manner which will emphasise their positive aspects. Fundamental to the success of such planning is a comprehensive approach which takes into account the extension of utilities and community facilities to transitional areas and the location of such areas in relation to transport networks and work places. This means breaking down administrative barriers and the traditional sectoral approach to planning and development, at all levels.

To establish a base for effective long-term policies, governments should institute a national assessment of the nature and extent of transitional settlements, of their estimated future growth and change and of their positive and negative effects on development: all this being aimed at determining more clearly the degree to which the forces resulting in their growth are a long-term concern. Governments should also analyse and evaluate the effectiveness of current programmes for low-income urban settlements and in particular the range of benefits that can accrue to such settlements from public spending decisions. These steps should be initiated immediately without prejudicing the development of short-term policies and programmes.

The will, ability and effectiveness with which governments develop short-term and long-term policies and programmes depend on a clear understanding of the problem and of the results of previous measures intended to deal with it. Unfortunately, present knowledge about transitional areas is far from clear and precise. A large number of case studies and government actions are well documented, but generally speaking transitional-settlement dwellers are not covered by official national records. There is no sizeable body of accurate data which would facilitate the development of national programmes and allow clear and detailed international comparisons of the nature, size and growth trends of transitional settlements and of the effect on them of current policies and programmes and of national planning decisions. High priority should therefore be given to developing a flow of more accurate information.

Planning measures should concentrate on the problems which the people concerned cannot solve for themselves, particularly the anticipation of the land-use needs of transitional-settlement growth and the planning and development of community services and infrastructure, both for existing settlements and for anticipated ones. A programme of land acquisition in advance of need should be designed to facilitate the extension of normal urban services to future transitional settlements, while preventing them from hindering the development of other necessary parts of the urban structure. Security of land tenure should be attainable within the means of the lowest-income groups, in locations accessible to jobs and integrated with the urban plan.

One measure which has proved effective, and is worthy of wider application, is the 'site and service' scheme under which the authorities acquire urban land in advance of need, plan for its eventual connection to the existing urban infrastructure, and make it available to low-income families as building sites equipped with the minimum services essential for health and access.

It is particularly important that from the outset the planning process should be designed and employed in a way which will draw a positive response from the inhabitants of transitional areas and facilitate the most efficient use of their own resources. But since the task that these people are least able to carry out for themselves is the planning of their settlements in relation to the urban area of which they form a part, it is essential that governments should take the initiative in this field, in order both to alleviate conditions in the short term and to speed improvements in the long term. In this way they will maximise the use of popular resources and help to prevent the growth of settlements in areas and patterns that preclude their eventual integration into a healthy urban system.

It is considerably cheaper, as well as generally more desirable, to underpin the process of progressive improvement by buying and preparing land for settlement rather than to attempt complete rehousing schemes. Even so, governments may wish to investigate the possibility of minimising their initial capital investment by the use of credit. The United Nations Centre for Housing, Building and Planning can assist and advise governments in planning. In addition, the World Health Organisation (WHO), the International Bank for Reconstruction and Development (IBRD), and the World Food Programme (WFP) have shown interest in this field.

The authorities concerned should establish reception programmes to help migrants to accelerate their adjustment to the demands of urban life and their integration into the urban community. Special training programmes should be instituted for both transitional-area inhabitants and government staff in the relevant aspects of public health, community development, building techniques and the formation of co-operatives, improvement associations and other local institutions. A dialogue should be established between the authorities and the community in the formulation of plans and procedures for joint action, particularly in relation to the building by the community of schools and other facilities which must fit into the official staffing and administrative structure.

Conscious participation and co-operation with the

authorities by the residents is fundamental and forms a vital part of their adjustment to urban life and training in citizenship. The provision of community facilities can be expected to stimulate participation, since there is ample evidence that settlers place a high priority on health, education and other social services. In this sphere also international help is available: from the United Nations Educational, Scientific and Cultural Organisation in relation to education and training; from the World Health Organisation for public health training and the development of health care facilities; from the Food and Agricultural Organisation for training in home economics and from the United Nations Children's Fund for the education and training of children and young people. The United Nations Centre for Housing, Building and Planning can provide training on various aspects of housing, building and planning, the United Nations Social Development Division on community development and social services and the International Labour Office (ILO) on vocational training.

Finding the Money
In both transitional-settlement and conventional housing, developing countries need improved financial machinery. While in many cases institutions such as building and loan societies exist to mobilise savings for housing, they are forced to ration their slender resources by charging high interest rates. In addition, they generally lack the backing of governmental mechanisms such as mortgage insurance, local secondary mortgage markets, central mortgage banks and government bond issues for housing. The introduction of such machinery often needs international aid in the form either of technical assistance or of capital investment from bilateral or multilateral lending agencies. Such assistance has not yet been attempted to any great extent in Africa or Asia, but has been relatively successful in establishing savings institutions and related financial mechanisms in Latin America, though the financial resources that may be available for such investment have probably not been fully tapped.

International funds, in combination with national resources, can be used as seed capital, not to build houses but to build institutions which in turn will mobilise national resources to finance the building and sale of houses and repay the international capital. But such measures can serve only a small proportion of the population of developing countries – those with sufficient income to cover mortgage repayments. An essential instrument for solving housing problems in developing countries must therefore be the development of techniques by which either international or local capital, or a combination of the two, can be used to stimulate, mobilise and channel the potential resources of low-income groups – the popular sector. For example, national housing finance institutions might extend long-term loans at subsidised rates to small credit co-operatives or unions organised by local communities. The credit co-operatives in turn could make small short-term loans at slightly higher rates for housing improvements. Only those who became members of the co-operatives by depositing a certain amount of savings would qualify for the loans. The interest-rate differential would allow the co-operative to repay the original loan and continue to mobilise the savings of the community.

Such arrangements have the advantage that the borrower would not be dealing with some impersonal bureaucracy or central mortgage bank but with his own friends, neighbours or relatives, who would know his means. Finally, and perhaps most significant for the urban environment, if the borrowers were required to choose from a selection of home improvement plans their financial, physical and organisational resources would be channelled towards a heterogeneous but orderly process of environmental improvement within official guidelines. This process could then be related to investment in other sectors – health, education, industry and so on – and integrated with various other kinds of house building.

International Aid

There are three main ways of mobilising national resources in developing countries which warrant international attention: (1) the fostering of international financial mechanisms to increase the flow of capital to savings banks, building societies, housing co-operatives and the like in the countries concerned; (2) the creation of non-profit-making joint development corporations offering an international career service and chartered to perform institution-building services in developing countries; (3) massive international training, research and development projects in the developed and developing countries designed to promote technological breakthroughs and to provide the new professional skills needed in the developing world. These three measures should be linked together in a comprehensive joint approach by the international community and the developing nations. Such steps would require an unprecedented concentration and co-ordination of resources and efforts at international and national levels.

At the international level there is a great need to strengthen and co-ordinate the efforts of various governmental, non-governmental and private bodies concerned with the housing environment. At the national level governments must make a determined effort to deal with their housing and urbanisation problems and to allocate resources in a consistent way to the housing sector, in keeping with the dynamics of development in each national economy. The target should be an allocation of at least 5 per cent of national income to finance housing and urban development — a substantial increase over existing levels in many developing countries but still far below the average level in advanced countries. They must establish national housing agencies to carry out continuous building programmes and must pay attention to all the possible means of lowering the cost of housing.

There must be a close relationship between programmes for promoting and mobilising savings and mechanisms for investing such savings in development. National governments can do much by themselves, and more if helped by international arrangements and guarantees, to stimulate and maintain the confidence of savers and investors. It should be remembered that many of the institutions which are lacking in developing countries and taken for granted in developed countries arose from humble origins and impoverished conditions. Necessity was the mother of invention for the weavers of Rochdale who founded the co-operative movement and for the organisers of the first savings banks, mortgage banks, building societies and credit unions. These forms of self-help and mutual help create a sound economic and social framework for sustained progress towards a fully satisfactory housing environment.

6 Industry

Industry and the Urban Environment
The industrial revolution of the nineteenth century profoundly changed the structure of society and transformed the
pattern of settlement in the now-developed countries. Men
were drawn from the land, the villages and the country towns
and concentrated in the new industrial cities which sprang up
near the sources of energy and raw materials. These cities
grew rapidly, because of the growing scale of industry and
the tendency for related industries to develop close to one
another, without regard for the environment. Although many
industries are now less tied to local sources of energy and raw
materials, and planning policies have secured a wider distribution of industrial plant, many of the early industrial cities
have continued to grow into densely populated conurbations,
often with a chaotic mixture of factories and tenements,
waste tips and remnants of agricultural land. Industrialisation
has brought with it economic expansion and rising standards
of living, increased consumption of goods and services and
increased environmental pollution.

In developing countries, however, the current rapid growth
of urban areas is not due primarily to industrialisation. Most
of the exploding cities are ports or administrative centres
which have attracted poor people from rural areas, usually to
live in appalling environmental conditions and without
sufficient job opportunities. In these circumstances industrial
development is needed to provide employment and support
the cost of building the infrastructure which is essential to a
better quality of life. Concentration of industries, however,
produces severe environmental pressures and conflicts; comprehensive planning, therefore, is needed to create the
optimal conditions for economic growth and social development and at the same time to protect and enhance the
environment.

Within these cities the location of industry must be

planned in relation to the other components — commercial and shopping centres, residential districts, open space and recreational areas, transport and other infrastructural systems. The need to have industrial areas close to residential districts in order to keep travel-to-work times as low as possible must be weighed against the need to protect residential areas from the atmospheric pollution and noise of industry. Special attention should be paid to the location of particularly noxious industries: the prevailing wind direction has an important influence on the area affected by air pollutants, smells and noises.

In the early stages of industrial development factory wastes produce only minor impacts on the environment, which the regulatory and self-healing mechanisms of the biosphere are capable of handling. With increasing amounts and concentrations of pollution the self-healing thresholds are passed and eventually so far exceeded that the life-sustaining processes of nature are destroyed. In the industrially advanced areas, where the scale of operations and rates of consumption continue to rise and the materials and processes become increasingly complex, these thresholds are passed more and more often. The developing countries are fortunate in having industrial operations which are still well below the safety limits — a situation they must take advantage of by learning from the past mistakes of the developed world and taking steps to control the adverse consequences and side-effects of industrialisation before they reach critical dimensions.

Industrial processes produce a wide variety of air-pollutants, many of which are dangerous to health either directly or through the effect on the micro-climate of their concentration in the atmosphere. Heating and power generation are largely dependent on the burning of fossil fuels, which produce smoke, soot and sulphur dioxide unless the combustion process is carefully controlled. Metal smelting, chemical and petrochemical industries generate a number of specific pollutants. Food industries, chemical industries, pulp and paper mills and many other types of processing plant produce liquid effluent which pollutes water courses. Solid wastes cause environmental problems either through their sheer volume — as in many mining processes — or through their toxicity. The disposal of chemical waste in particular demands care, since the potential hazard may not be immediately apparent. This has happened in the dumping at sea of scrap plastic-coated wires containing polychlorinated phenyls — stable compounds which became concentrated in marine food chains and adversely affected sea birds.

Governments are increasingly requiring industry to control environmental disturbances through compliance with stringent standards and enforcement measures, which often involve heavy capital expenditure on equipment. However, new processes may result in reduced emissions, sometimes as the unintended side-effect of the more efficient use of materials. Developing countries where new industries are being planned often have a choice of several newly developed processes: these should be carefully evaluated in terms of environmental disturbance as well as of more conventional costs and benefits. A process which has a higher initial cost may yield long-term benefits when the costs of pollution control, or of suffering the consequences of pollution, are taken into account.

Industrial projects should be evaluated in terms of their costs and benefits to the whole community, including environmental costs. Some of these cost factors can be assessed fairly easily. Standards can be set for clean air and water and the costs to the community of various measures to achieve these standards can be calculated. Similarly the costs of neglecting them can also be assessed, although in this case the calculations are often more difficult and involve factors that are hard to quantify. It is even more difficult to put a cost on a reduced quality of life in terms of social pressures, deterioration in health and well-being and visual squalor, but economists and sociologists are giving increasing attention to these issues. What is abundantly clear is that the simple cost-benefit analysis which neglects all social and environmental repercussions is inadequate and misleading.

It is clear also that the community will increasingly expect industry to meet at least part of the cost of the environmental disturbance it causes. In this context it is important to remember that it is usually cheaper to design pollution-control techniques as an integral part of the plant than to take remedial measures afterwards. It is also important that the magnitude of industry's contribution to environmental pollution should be set in perspective. The collective effect on the residential environment of motor vehicles and other non-industrial sources of pollution and disturbance probably outweighs that of industry.

Urban planning should involve balanced development between industrial, commercial and residential areas and open spaces. This is not a simple matter to achieve. There are conflicting needs and interests to be considered and compromises to be struck. The locational demands of industry, including the need for some industries to be close together and to have good access to transportation systems, must be weighed against environmental considerations and the need for the urban system as a whole to function efficiently and effectively.

Increasing attention is being paid to the location of industry in relation to recreational space and to areas of natural beauty and scientific interest. No longer can industry count on hugging shorelines and river banks, for these places are increasingly at a premium for recreation and housing; it must expect to be set further back and separated from waterfronts by green belts. The visual appearance of industrial areas is another important matter, and one of which industrialists are becoming increasingly aware. Engineers and architects can collaborate to make the environment of the industrial plant pleasing and harmonious. A parkland or garden setting, together with well-designed buildings and carefully chosen colours, materials and lighting, can make a workplace pleasant and attractive to workers and passers-by alike.

Industrial Location
The extent to which the location of industry is determined by physical planning varies from country to country. Where socialisation of the economic system is more fully developed the influence of physical planning in this field is strong. In countries with high levels of economic development and per capita consumption it is easier for planners to induce

industry to take account of non-economic considerations when deciding on the location of new projects. Where land suitable for industry is relatively scarce, as in Switzerland, the land-use pattern has become a critical factor in physical planning. In these various situations the traditional attitude of physical planners has been to consider primarily the negative consequences of industrial development — pollution and the destruction of aesthetic values — and to formulate zoning laws to regulate the impact of industry on human settlements.

At the regional level the planner's attitude to industry is mainly influenced by the stage of development of the region in question. In 'weak' regions the main objective is to attract industry to the region to provide jobs and stimulate economic growth. In 'strong' regions the planner has to consider the growing social costs of continuing industrial development. In these already highly industrialised areas the added cost of controlling pollution and mitigating environmental disturbances can be a decisive factor in judging the desirability of new industrial projects. The greater the environmental pressure, the less desirable additional industry is likely to be. Developing countries, which are 'weak' in these terms, may be able to profit from this situation. With their current industrial activity at relatively low levels, they are often well below the threshold at which environmental pressures become of paramount importance. They offer the opportunity of establishing new industry without causing serious environmental damage.

Modern industry has a number of basic locational needs. There must be good communications to facilitate the flow of materials and finished goods. Water, drainage, electricity and other services must be available at reasonable costs. In addition to the physical infrastructure, there must be an adequate financial infrastructure, including fiscal incentives and access to money markets. Technical and professional services must be available. These factors, together with the basic need for access to markets, raw materials and labour, determine the best locations for the development of particular industries. They are often the decisive reasons for the continued concentration of industry in large cities. In this context there are two other subtle but important considerations: the emphasis given in business dealings to face-to-face meetings and the personal preference of many managers and technicians for living in or near large cities.

These factors must be borne in mind in considering ways of achieving the planned redistribution of population and industry which is of particular importance in developing countries. A genuine economic and social revival of depressed rural areas can succeed only through the creation of new growth centres which will give the necessary impetus to a redistribution of industrial activities. These growth centres must be carefully chosen and planned to make effective use of land and resources and to avoid any repetition of the uncontrolled growth that has been the cause of so many current problems. In this connection the creation of industrial estates equipped with all the necessary infrastructural facilities is a useful device. It reduces the investment required by individual enterprises and thereby stimulates new industrial development. At the same time it helps to get industry located according to plan within the urban areas.

In developing countries at an early stage of industrialisation, the promotion in rural areas of small-scale industries that do not make excessive demands on capital equipment and managerial skills is a good way of providing employment and stimulating economic growth. Industries based on processing agricultural products are particularly suited to this kind of location. There can be a saving in transport costs where this sort of industry is close to the source of raw materials, since the finished product is usually much less bulky than the raw materials.

The Building Industry

There is something of a special relationship between the building industry and the environment. On the one hand, it is a significant source of both long-term environmental damage and of short-term pollution and disturbance; on the other, it creates the major components of the man-made environment.

Although building has always been an important human activity its damaging impact on the environment is a comparatively recent phenomenon. Before the advent of modern technologies and the rapid growth of settlements, building activity seldom had an intolerable impact on the environment and the disturbance it caused was always temporary. Buildings generally harmonised with their natural surroundings. In such areas building materials are produced mostly by artisans or on a semi-industrial scale, and the environmental impact of their production is localised or insignificant, consisting mainly of the spoliation and dereliction of land by quarrying and the depletion of timber resources by their use either for firing bricks and lime or as a building material. Disturbance on this scale can be fairly easily counteracted by controlling the exploitation of raw materials and insisting on land reclamation and re-afforestation.

In developed regions the rapid increase in the rate of building activity, combined with the advent of mass-production techniques, mechanised processes and new materials, has greatly magnified the impact of the building industry in all its aspects — the winning of raw materials, the manufacture of components and the construction of buildings and civil engineering works. This impact has been aggravated by the tendency, wherever raw material supplies permit, to concentrate quarrying, processing and manufacturing in and around large settlements. In particular the ever-increasing use of concrete has resulted in the indiscriminate exploitation of readily available sources of sand, gravel and stone in the vicinity of large settlements throughout the world, leading to widespread destruction of landscapes which can be restored only at great cost.

With the exhaustion of resources close to big towns, building materials industries are gradually developing in places often quite remote from their main markets. This trend is also stimulated by the demand from civil engineering works scattered throughout any country and the growth in the requirements of rural areas and small settlements resulting from higher standards of living. However, the distribution of these industries in most countries remains uneven, overtaxing the environment of large settlements and adding to the pollution and nuisance caused by other industries.

A number of specific nuisances caused by building

industries may be noted. Cement factories, even when technologically advanced, are a major source of air pollution by comparison with other building industries and with industry generally. The pollutants include waste gases from fuel — which may be reduced if gas or oil with a low sulphur content is used — and dust. Even if the dust has only a marginal effect on human health because of its low content of siliceous compounds, it remains a serious nuisance. One medium-sized cement works of an old-fashioned design and with poor dust control equipment may deposit as much as 1000 tons per square kilometre of dust each year. The dust-fall may affect an area up to five kilometres from the factory or even further, depending on the prevailing winds. Modern equipment may reduce the dust pollution to 0.1 per cent of the volume of cement production, or even less; but it is expensive, increasing the total investment by 10 per cent or more. Technical measures are, of course, ineffective if managements fail to make proper use of them, as often happens.

The production of building lime causes noise and pollutes the air with sulphur dioxide and dust, both of which can be reduced by the use of suitable fuels and equipment. The manufacture of clay bricks and tiles, ceramics and glass also causes air pollution. Most of these industries depend to a greater or lesser extent on the nearby quarrying of raw materials, which spoils the land, generates air pollution, dust and noise and is unsightly. A number of quarrying processes, including the washing of concrete aggregates and the treatment of kaolin and glass-sand, result in significant water pollution. Airborne fibres of asbestos released in processing are a serious health hazard. Modern equipment, adequate regulations, strict supervision and the careful location of quarries can reduce, but not entirely eliminate, these harmful effects.

It is debatable whether the environmental impact of quarrying is best controlled by concentrating operations in a few large units (where the size of deposits makes this possible) or by dispersing them throughout the country in many small units. Large units offer economies of scale and are more easily supervised by public authorities, but their extensive blasting operations and the concentrated use of excavators, drills, compressors, bulldozers and trucks may cause serious disturbance within a five-kilometre radius.

Whatever the pattern adopted, quarrying and associated manufacturing processes should be prohibited close to settlements and recreational areas. All quarrying should be licensed and the restoration of the land immediately after the end of operations should be obligatory. In addition, close public supervision should be exercised to prevent the reckless exploitation of mineral reserves. Sometimes high-quality minerals, including pure limestone, special ceramic clays, pure kaolin, asbestos and other materials are used in products for which lower-quality materials of a similar type are perfectly adequate, with the result that reserves are prematurely exhausted.

In the case of cement the argument for locating factories at some distance from urban areas is supported by the economics of the industry. Cement is generally a very cheap material, averaging $10 to $20 a ton at building sites in developed countries. In most urban building activities cement represents only one or two per cent of the total cost. Thus transportation, which is invariably a significant cost factor, is not particularly critical in the urban context. On the other hand it is usually a decisive cost factor in civil engineering works such as dams and highways. Moreover, cement factories do not create employment opportunities of any real significance in urban areas: a modern plant of about 500,000 tons annual output employs 200 or fewer workers.

The building industry is one of the main consumers of timber, and often a wasteful one. In several parts of the world where timber felling has not been followed by re-afforestation, barren wastes remain as a witness to human greed and recklessness. Even in regions where timber resources are seemingly inexhaustible, a greater use of plywood and composition boards made from less valuable timber species and from sawdust and chippings should be encouraged to help to conserve forests.

Noise from a wide variety of machinery and operations is probably the most obnoxious side-effect of building work in urban areas. Although it is well known that any sound over

80 decibels is uncomfortable, that over 90 decibels may be harmful to health and that over 100 decibels can cause permanent loss of hearing, we have become resigned to noise levels of around 90 decibels or more on building sites. It is impossible to eliminate noise on building sites completely, but a number of measures can be taken to reduce noise and the impact of noise without requiring a significant modification of building technologies and economics. Some essential machinery, particularly compressors, can be muffled, and some can be powered by electricity rather than combustion engines. Non-emergency building operations which generate noise can be prohibited at night. Employers can be obliged to provide building workers with ear plugs. Maximum use can be made of prefabricated components and ready-mixed concrete, and repairs to equipment and machinery can be done away from the site. The work programme can be designed and managed to reduce noise and to speed up the completion of the work. Building regulations, strictly enforced, are needed to achieve noise reductions by these means.

The environmental impact of large-scale engineering works outside urban areas can be many-sided and far-reaching, particularly when the works are carried out in remote and sparsely populated areas where few people are directly and immediately affected and public pressure for the protection of the environment is consequently less strong. The construction of dams, highways, railroads and airports not only removes large areas of land from agriculture but may also sterilise large adjoining areas of land which could be recultivated if the developers were subjected to appropriate control. Where large expanses of land are paved, the run-off of rainwater may deplete natural underground reservoirs. Developments of this kind may also affect the microclimate — sometimes beneficently, sometimes adversely — and interfere with plant and wildlife regimes. In addition the visual impact of such large developments should be carefully considered in relation to the natural landscape. Structures which may be architecturally or technically impressive as human achievements may rest uneasily in their natural setting.

Policy Issues

A number of national policies to counteract the environmental impact of building industries are indicated by the issues considered above. Building regulations and other legislative and administrative measures affecting building activities and the production of building materials should be revised and extended to prevent or reduce noise pollution and other nuisances. The use of prefabricated components and off-site services for building operations should be encouraged, promoted and, if need be, subsidised by public authorities. Public supervision of building operations should be intensified and the nuisances they cause should be taken into account in their planning, particularly in the case of redevelopment schemes. The establishment within urban areas of building materials factories that cause serious pollution problems should be prohibited. Means of eliminating pollution should be sought when production units are being designed rather than after they have been built.

In respect of industry generally, two main approaches to the problem of pollution and environmental damage warrant careful examination. One is the development or adoption of new technologies which reduce pollution and other undesirable side-effects; the second is the location of new industrial plants in areas where there is not already a large concentration of industry and the environment therefore retains its capacity to absorb and dispose of pollutants. The prospect of helping the economic growth of developing nations through such measures is another consideration which requires the attention of policy-makers.

The environmental problems of industrial development can be tackled only if there is an effective land-use planning system to ensure that industries are properly located in the light of environmental issues. Planners should consider specifically the question of what constitutes an optimum concentration of industry, together with the possibility of establishing new enterprises in underdeveloped regions or of transferring existing enterprises to them from highly industrialised regions.

Measures are also needed to abate pollution and other nuisances where industries are already concentrated. These may include tax reliefs and other incentives to the adoption of alternative technologies which reduce environmental disturbance, methods of treating effluent and emissions and methods of re-cycling waste products. Pollution may be penalised by taxation provided there is an adequate system for monitoring the output of pollutants.

The report of the study of critical environmental problems sponsored by the Massachusetts Institute of Technology[1] summarises the types of remedial action that can be taken by industry. These include: (1) changes in raw materials; (2) changes in energy sources; (3) changes in production, including the adoption of different processes, the re-cycling and absorption or alternative treatment of wastes; (4) changes in end-product; and (5) changes in the quantity of the end-product used. Tax reliefs and penalties and other concessions and regulations can be designed to induce the adoption of such remedial measures.

7   Leisure

Introduction

Mankind everywhere has a basic biological need for the regeneration of body and spirit which comes from various forms of recreation. In developed countries where rapid economic growth is meeting most material needs there is a growing demand for greater and more diversified opportunities for recreation. The use of labour-saving devices in industry and commerce and in the home leaves people with more free time but simultaneously tends to make work monotonous and unsatisfying. It becomes all the more important that they should be able to use their leisure to replenish their physical, psychological and emotional energies.

The increase in leisure and the general rise in the level of culture have changed the social content and significance of recreation. For many people an ever-increasing part of their leisure is spent, not simply in restoring their capacity for work, but in satisfying personal needs and interests. At least some of these needs and interests must be satisfied in the open air in a variety of ways and places.

Open Space in Urban Areas

Open space kept in a natural state contributes to the welfare of settlements in three ways: it provides an opportunity for people to enjoy their leisure in physically and spiritually satisfying surroundings; it provides a break in the continuity of built-up areas and a visual contrast to them; and it constitutes a natural ventilation system which helps to counteract the changes caused in the atmosphere by the presence of settlements. All three are essential components in the environment of human settlements.

The demands for recreation correspond broadly with the rhythms of working life. People need opportunities for daily recreation close to their homes and workplaces, for longer periods at week-ends at a moderate distance from the home

and for annual holidays in distant places in their own country
or abroad. Only a complete hierarchy of provision can meet
all the needs.

Daily needs are met by small parks, playgrounds, allot-
ments and footpath systems in residential areas; by open
spaces and playing fields for lunch-time and after-work
recreation in industrial areas; and by parks, squares and
greenways in central areas. The form, character and amount
of open space required will vary considerably in accordance
with the surrounding land uses. Low-density residential areas
with big private gardens need less public open space than
high-density housing areas. In densely built-up urban centres
there is need for town squares, of which the archetype is the
Square of St Mark in Venice. In many other great cities and
small towns open markets have survived as squares. Although
today the forms and uses of buildings in central areas have
changed, the need for such spaces remains so that people may
walk, sit and talk or buy and sell without the risk of being
run over by a car. Cities like Paris demonstrate that even a
small space with a few trees and two or three seats can play
an important part in meeting the need for open space.

In the city as a whole the needs of residents and visitors
are met by larger parks with picnic areas, walks, bridle and
cycle paths and play areas; by playing-fields for team sports;
and by botanical gardens and zoos. Ideally, small and large
open spaces in cities should be connected by systems of
footpaths and greenways to one another and outward to
regional parks or green belts. Recreation areas surrounding
cities have to be related to existing agricultural systems and
there may be conflicts of interest which can only be resolved
by political decisions. Greater London is fortunate that its
green belt lies in an area of dairy farming and sheep rearing
which can accommodate day visitors from the city. The
problem becomes more difficult where the land is arable: in
the Netherlands there is often an acute conflict between the
recreational needs of city people and the intensive cultivation
of the land.

A great variety of open air provision can be made for
visitors, holiday-makers and tourists in the countryside away
from the cities, in river valleys and hill country, mountains

and coastal areas, in the form of small and large regional parks, national parks and nature reserves, with facilities for fishing, hiking, riding, boating and driving along scenic routes. Some will meet mainly regional needs, others national and international needs. Here again the needs of recreation have to be harmonised with the needs of agriculture, forestry and water catchment by good planning and management.

Recreation Planning and Management
Each country will have its own concept of an open-space system appropriate to its social and economic objectives. The character of open spaces depends a great deal on climatic conditions. In temperate countries with even rainfall it is assumed almost automatically that recreation areas will consist largely of grassy parkland. This model is, of course, unrealistic in climates with low rainfall or in monsoon areas where the vegetation responds to severe climatic changes during the year. The depth of topsoil may be an important factor also — countries like Sweden are accustomed to making use of rocky outcroppings with thin soil which occur in, for instance, the Stockholm area.

There can be no 'international style' in recreational areas and provisions. The use made of leisure is unique to each culture. Recreation areas and facilities must always be designed to fit local customs, social structure and climate and not the preconceptions or convenience of experts. Individual countries, and even regions within countries, have their own priorities and values to be served. When facilities are provided that no one wants to use, scarce resources of money, time and energy have been wasted. Thus studies carried out as the basis of planning must seek to establish the kind as well as the amount of provision that is needed. Consultation with the people to be served, both to learn their wishes and to explain the alternatives available, can help to ensure that the provision meets the real demand. Anthropological and sociological field studies can also assist in this respect.

Estimating the need for recreation areas and open spaces in relation to the total population, the density of population in specific places, the categories of people with different needs, interests and incomes and the demand at local, regional and national levels is a most difficult problem. Not enough research has been done in developed countries, let alone developing countries, to produce a generally applicable system of measuring these needs. There are problems too in putting a value on open space. The standards we have for assessing the value of human happiness and fulfilment are primitive indeed compared with those we can command for assessing industrial output. So the investment priorities go elsewhere and a destructive cycle begins. Urban lands are developed for housing, industry, commerce, services and transport at high and increasing densities. What open space there is tends to become grossly over-used, to the point where it loses most of its value. In some cities recreation areas are often dusty wastes completely devoid of vegetation. Often there is nowhere for children to play except mudflats and rubbish heaps. Even where the existing provision is adequate for present needs it may be insufficient to meet the demands of a growing population. But growth puts a premium on land and there is a temptation to let the pressure on existing recreation areas increase to and beyond the point of over-use.

The loss of existing open spaces is a constant problem. Many older cities have inherited open areas provided by rulers, governments and the rich. Many of these areas are being nibbled away to provide sites for schools, housing or highways and are fast disappearing. Where such land is taken for development, alternative open spaces should always be provided, but the creation of new open spaces and recreation areas inside older cities requires extraordinary amounts of determination and money. There are, however, various devices for squeezing out new open spaces in built-up areas.

In both developing and developed countries the basic issue is the same. Under the pressure to use land for more tangible rewards there is a great temptation to allocate for public open space only what is left over from other uses. Yet the prior allocation of open space in places where it will act as a boundary to guide development into predetermined zones can save money in the long run. For the main problem brought about by unplanned urban growth is the costly provision of infrastructures to widely scattered residential areas. This is a world-wide problem, but it is particularly acute in developing countries, where massive migration from rural areas has led to the growth of unplanned squatter settlements. The initial pattern in which these transitional urban settlements become established is commonly the single most pervasive and inflexible factor affecting their growth and improvement. Such areas generally lack even the most elementary amenities and public space for recreation is an unheard-of luxury. It is all the more difficult to clear space when this will deprive people of their homes.

If as much stress is placed on the planning of open spaces as on the planning of residential, industrial and commercial areas, harmony can be achieved between the natural and man-made components of the environment without delaying development or increasing its costs. Only by comprehensive planning can the relationship between housing, industry, transport and recreation be recognised and acted upon and land secured for public use before it becomes too costly. A hierarchy of interconnected spaces planned throughout the urban area can help to reduce the long-term monetary cost of urban growth by contributing to a more efficient and appropriate pattern of land uses and transport systems.

Besides providing opportunities for recreation, open spaces provide light and air for buildings, particularly the closely packed and tall buildings of city centres. They also relieve congestion and afford privacy, sound insulation and a sense of spaciousness.

A long-term regional comprehensive plan for open-space provision should state the goals and objectives to be achieved; should map all the sites, showing their topography, climate, geology and ecology; and should present a strategy for implementing the plan, including financial provisions and procedures for the acquisition or designation of land for various recreational and open-space uses. The advance designation of sites is important since it notifies other agencies that the sites are not available for schools, hospitals, community services and other forms of development.

A number of basic principles should be observed. Proposed facilities should be harmoniously related to existing environmental qualities; the soil, air and water should be protected from pollution, and the recreation areas from blight, noise and other nuisances generated by traffic and industry; open spaces should be designed to improve the micro-climate; special features of the landscape should be protected against destruction and from aesthetic pollution by haphazard development; the sites should be designed in such a way that their continuing quality and usefulness is assured; and provision should be made for their management.

Land which is unsuitable for development or needs protection from development can be designated as public open space. Such areas include river valleys liable to flooding, groundwater recharge areas, marshes and swamps, steep hillsides and areas with unique natural ecological communities which should be protected for their scientific value.

One useful exercise in cost-benefit analysis which most city authorities might undertake is to assume that all vacant lands and existing recreational areas are developed with housing, industry, commerce and transport systems: after the benefits of such development have been measured the costs in terms of congestion, overcrowding, dirty air and loss of natural landscape can be weighed against them.

The use made of public recreation areas must be carefully controlled if their physical quality and recreational value are to be maintained. If too many people use a recreation area they will simply destroy the qualities which brought them there in the first place. The problem has two dimensions. In physical terms, too many people crowding into a park or playing-field will damage the land, trampling down the soil until it is washed away or blown away and breaking off or wearing down vegetation. The concept of a carrying capacity, or limit to the number of people who can use the area daily, seasonally or annually without damaging its ecosystem, is beginning to be applied to the management of parks and recreation areas. This capacity will depend upon the ecological status of the site, its capacity to regenerate itself after use and the spatial and temporal pattern of public use.

The recreational value of a site may also depend upon the number of users at any one time or the kinds of activity carried on at the same time. A quiet small park enjoyed by local residents, particularly older people who cannot walk or

travel far to seek their recreation, may lose its value to them
if it comes to be used by large numbers of noisy children.
Similarly a wilderness used by people who value its solitude
and the sense of communion with nature will lose its value to
these people if it becomes intensively used. The amount of
use that is psychologically damaging may be below the
threshold where significant physical damage is done. In
contrast, if an open space or square in a busy business district
or densely settled residential area was not heavily used
because it was inadequately policed or otherwise considered
dangerous or unattractive, it would not achieve its purpose;
for the value of such areas lies in the animation aroused by
large numbers of people carrying on a variety of activities.

Once the commitment is made to reserve land for
recreation there must be an equally strong commitment to its
management. Well-trained and dedicated people are needed
to carry out this task. To ensure proper management, the
powers to acquire and manage recreational areas should be
vested in the same agency.

Planning for Tourists

Recreation is increasingly an international activity. Greater
personal wealth and leisure and easier travel are turning a
growing number of people into tourists. Tourism as an
important instrument for fostering and maintaining international good-will. It is also an economically productive
enterprise benefiting all sectors of society in tourist areas by
stimulating building and the provision of improved infrastructure and by increasing job opportunities in service occupa-
tions. But tourists in great numbers in a concentrated period
of time can destroy the attractions they come in search of.
Every natural beauty spot and historic shrine has a capacity
which can become saturated, and the more attractive it is, the
more likely it is to be damaged by over-use.

Long-range comprehensive planning of tourist regions is
needed to control the number of visitors and to make
efficient and effective use of public investment in roads,
hotels, camping sites and other facilities. Many countries are
already developing comprehensive national policies for the
controlled exploitation of tourist areas and there is a growing

body of experience in preparing and implementing national and regional plans. The main issues a tourist development plan has to resolve centre on the quality, quantity and location of facilities and supporting services. These in turn determine the kinds of tourist attracted, in terms of income and interests, the mode of transport by which they arrive and depart, and the length of their stay. Each of these factors has a direct bearing on the degree to which preserving and maintaining the original qualities of the environment is feasible.

Environmental qualities of special value should be assessed at the outset of the planning process. The elements to be inventoried and evaluated for each area include its location, geology and seismology, topography, water supply, landscape and climate. Whether its current population is sufficient to support tourist facilities and services must also be assessed, together with the level of its economic development and its pattern of land use and transport, for all these factors will influence its capacity to provide services of the kind that attract tourists and satisfy their needs.

Particular attention should be paid to basic health measures, including the provision of water supplies and drainage and waste disposal systems, the qualitative control of water and food and the sanitary inspection of hotels, restaurants and tourist camps.

To exemplify the matters requiring analysis and decision when developing tourist facilities in an area of scenic, natural and historic value, we refer to the Master Plan[1] for the development of the island of Hvar, off the coast of Yugoslavia. Hvar has a beautiful seashore and several villages of great charm. The Regional Plan for the Adriatic Shore shows Western Hvar as one of thirteen areas proposed for comprehensive tourist development. The special character of the island is recognised as most suitable for people seeking the quieter and more secluded kind of holiday, and for those making visits for the sake of their health, especially in winter. The Regional Plan guidelines also specify the need for concentrated development, for the revival of historic towns and for protection of the landscape.

Analysing the characteristics of the island which have

guided the development proposals, the Master Plan describes it as a seemingly remote but easily accessible place with an atmosphere of 'somewhere special'. It emphasises the peace and tranquillity of the island and its variety of landscape within a small radius, drawing attention to the land-locked bays with sheltered beaches surrounded by pine-covered hills, the well-preserved medieval and renaissance cores of the towns, which are 'excellent examples of some of the most civilised forms of human settlement', and the continuity of life from prehistoric times to the present day, which has 'left a rich cultural heritage that the visitor can explore in the monuments surviving from every period'. It stresses the Mediterranean climate, which is suitable for winter tourism and for people suffering from respiratory diseases. It concludes that the island could offer a wealth of recreational activities within a small area — sailing and other water sports, swimming, fishing, sun-bathing, donkey trekking and shooting.

It is necessary to determine what types of tourist can enjoy these attractions to the full without damaging the resources on which they are based, the Plan says. Tourists, it goes on, can be classified in several ways: according to their mode of travel, whether they come independently or in groups, their national origin, demographic characteristics and motive for travel. 'The last of these aspects, though the most difficult to classify and measure, is probably the most relevant to our problem', it adds.

The Plan continues:

Two broad groups may be distinguished. The majority of holiday-makers who make up the mass market at present seek five basic amenities — sunshine, beaches, pleasant accommodation, some evening entertainment and a quick and convenient journey. Their choice of resort tends to be determined by relative costs. A minority of selective tourists seek these five basic amenities plus other attractions, e.g., scenery, history, folklore, sport. While relative costs are important to many of them, their choice of resort is also strongly influenced by the special amenities offered.

The distinctive personality of Western Hvar would be

endangered by a big increase in the number of private cars and in the amount of road space ... the number of visitors' cars in the Master Plan area at any one time should not exceed 3800. The reasoning is briefly as follows: both financial and aesthetic considerations limit the total length of roads that can be provided and their prevailing width; traffic should not be the maximum these roads can safely carry but a lower amount giving the opportunity of relaxed driving and enjoyment of the scenery, and avoiding any appearance of congestion ... the number of cars must therefore be controlled by limiting the capacity of the ferry services. Suitable pricing policies, booking arrangements and publicity must be devised to prevent congestion and long queues at the mainland ferry terminals. Motorists should be encouraged to leave their cars at Split and spend some time on Hvar, and it should be made cheaper and more convenient to do this than to take cars to the island. This will require adequate, safe and sheltered car parks adjacent to the hydrofoil terminals at Split, with convenient arrangements for transferring baggage directly from cars on the mainland to hotels on the island.

The Plan divides the tourist accommodation on the island between camps and three categories of hotel, with three-quarters of it in middle-range hotels — which are the most profitable.

The Plan says that the very qualities that make Western Hvar unsuitable for mass tourism make it especially attractive to more selective tourists with special interests, whose number is likely to grow with the growth of incomes and leisure and rising standards of education. 'And with the increasingly rapid pace of urban life more may wish to spend their holidays in a place offering a complete contrast to their everyday surroundings.'

8 Infrastructure

The Vital Role of Water

A safe and adequate supply of water is a basic need of human life. A safe and adequate system for supplying and distributing water and for removing and treating soiled water is a basic need of the human settlement, an essential part of the infrastructure which supports it and enables it to function. In many settlements the public water supply and sewerage system is grossly inadequate even for present requirements, while the demand for water is constantly increasing with the growth of population and rises in the standard of living.

The water resources of any nation are an invaluable asset which must be preserved and maintained. In some countries, particularly in arid and semi-arid regions, the scarcity of natural water resources underlines the need for careful conservation. In other, highly-developed, countries even if water is naturally plentiful the sheer magnitude of the demand means that sources must be conserved, used water treated and re-cycled, and watercourses kept free from pollution and contamination.

Large areas of the world are virtually uninhabitable solely because it is impracticable or uneconomic to supply water in sufficient quantity or of adequate quality to support settlements. Not all of these areas are desert. In Africa there are tracts of seasonal grassland that support large herds of cattle tended by nomadic tribes. The humped cattle are able to go for long periods without water, while the tribesmen carry enough with them in goatskins to meet their minimal needs during the dry season. Where modern technology has made it possible to provide water supplies, as in the artificial hafirs in the Sudan and the deep boreholes in the Chad basin, settlements have formed. In consequence living standards rise, for health, education and other services can be provided where there is a stable population; the quality of the cattle improves because long migrations are no longer necessary;

and it becomes possible to develop better cattle markets and processing plants.

In other areas water is available but is too brackish for human consumption. In parts of the Euphrates valley, for instance, people are forced to settle along the river banks because the abundant groundwater has a high sulphur content. Thus areas which could support crops and settlements remain uninhabited. Modern technology can usually make this sort of water drinkable, although not necessarily at a price which is economically feasible. Improvements in technique may alter this situation. With increasing awareness of the role of water supply in opening up unproductive land, and a greater readiness on the part of financing agencies to support work of this nature, national programmes of groundwater development are likely to assume greater significance in years to come.

The demand for water, in terms of both quantity and quality, grows in stages. Primitive settlements simply want enough water to satisfy their basic requirements, and they are not over-particular about the quality. At a later stage of development the demand is for water that is free from the organisms that cause fatal and crippling diseases, while more advanced societies want water of high and carefully controlled quality, reasonably odourless, tasteless and colourless and free from toxic and other deleterious substances. Similarly, while the nomad or desert dweller can survive on a few litres of water a day, the villager wants a larger amount for domestic and agricultural use, and the townsman, particularly in industrialised countries, needs a hundred times as much for a wide variety of purposes: collectively for industry, commerce, horticulture, municipal hygiene, fire-fighting, recreation, and so on; individually for bathing, flushing toilets, laundry, central heating, washing the car, watering the garden — all the uses associated with a high standard of living.

While the migrant herdsman may be prepared to collect water and carry it with him, the villager in developing countries needs a more convenient supply from a village well or standpipe, and the sophisticated townsman wants water brought not only to his house but into his bedroom. Thus what is a necessity at one level is a luxury at another; and this is reflected in the willingness of the consumer to pay for what he receives. Simple access to water is regarded as a natural entitlement: by custom and religion, water is freely given and expected. The villager, who is more interested in the quantity, physical quality and convenience of the supply (which he understands) than in its bacterial or chemical purity (the significance of which is usually beyond his comprehension), may be willing to contribute to the cost of sinking a well or running a pump. In highly developed cities, where the implications of safe and adequate water supply are more fully appreciated, payment is customary for water that has been collected, treated, stored, pumped and distributed. The consumer knows that he is being asked to pay, not for the water itself, but for the processing and conveyance of it and for the provision of a reliable service.

Treatment and Supply
Existing water-supply systems are often far from adequate. The notion of a public water supply – an organised means of abstracting water from its source, treating it to improve the quality and distributing it to the consumer – is more often an ideal than a reality in developing countries. The World Health Organisation estimates that in 1970, in developing countries which were members of WHO, 25 per cent of townspeople had water piped to the house and 26 per cent used a public standpipe (the latter figure excludes Latin America where higher totals have been achieved). But less than 10 per cent of rural people were supplied with safe water. The WHO's targets for the United Nations Second Development Decade are to raise these figures to 40 per cent, 60 per cent and 20 per cent respectively by 1980.

External loans to developing countries for the construction of urban water systems in the period 1958 to 1970 amounted to some $950 million. Even when government contributions are added this represents only a quarter of the estimated expenditure needed to meet the 1980 targets. No figures are available for rural areas, but the present rate of progress is obviously too slow even to keep pace with population growth, let alone to make up the backlog.

At present, then, the great majority of people in developing countries get water whenever they can with the minimum of inconvenience and in ignorance of the dangers they are facing from contaminated and infected sources. In one Asian country it has been estimated that 60 per cent of all illness and 40 per cent of all deaths can be attributed to water-borne diseases. National statistics are hard to come by, but this may be by no means an unusual situation.

Several categories of disease are related to water, or the lack of it. Fatal diseases such as cholera, typhoid, infantile diarrhoea and other forms of dysentery, which are either endemic or occur as sporadic epidemics, are transmitted by water from the excreta of infected people to other people, either directly or through food. Debilitating diseases such as amoebic dysentery and guinea-worm disease (dracontiasis) are caused by the ingestion of water-borne parasites, while other parasitic diseases such as bilharzia (schistosomiasis) are associated with reservoirs and other water resource development schemes. Another class of diseases, including tropical ulcers, scabies, impetigo, yaws and trachoma is associated with lack of water for personal hygiene. In most developing countries such diseases constitute the main health problem. In addition they have considerable and diverse economic implications: the victims of debilitating diseases are unable to work; irrigation projects have had to be abandoned because they were spreading bilharzia; the presence of epidemic diseases discourages tourism; widespread ill-health nullifies educational and nutritional programmes and throws the burden of the blind and the crippled on to the local economy; and the risk of disease makes potentially productive land uninhabitable. To all these must be added the immense toll of human suffering. It is estimated that at all times there are 200 million people – one in fifteen of the world population – suffering from just one of these diseases: bilharzia.

In addition to bacteria and parasites, water sources may be contaminated by chemicals ranging in seriousness from poisons and carcinogens to substances of mild nuisance value affecting the taste or colour. As a general rule chemical contaminants are easier to detect but harder to remove than bacterial ones. Man-made chemical pollution is mainly a problem of highly industrialised societies. In developing countries the main problem at present is naturally-occurring minerals, but as industrialisation and the use of agricultural chemicals increase, the risk of man-made contamination increases too. These countries are less well equipped to detect and remove or to exclude such pollutants than the developed countries; but even the latter are finding that current techniques cannot cope with some of the new pollutants, and that surveillance, testing and treatment are becoming increasingly expensive and sophisticated.

There is usually not enough staff and equipment available, except in the largest cities, to monitor all the possible water pollutants. Moreover, conventional treatment systems will not remove many of the new contaminants, and systems that will are expensive to build and operate. It is better to remove contaminating substances at source whenever this is possible, but it is difficult enough to identify industrial sources and almost impossible to detect agricultural ones. If developing countries are to prevent the problem growing to unmanageable proportions they must take early steps to equip themselves with trained staff, facilities, legal safeguards and organisations. International aid is available to help them to do this, but governments must first recognise the existence of the problem and be willing to take the initiative.

To be effective a public water supply must be not only safe in quality but also sufficient in quantity and certain in delivery. If the supply is insufficient or intermittent people are forced to resort to other, unsafe sources, or to store water, often in insanitary containers. Moreover, a supply which is subject to changes in pressure is liable to contamination by infected groundwater. This is because leakages are inevitable in even the best distribution systems, and when the internal pressure falls groundwater may be siphoned into the pipes.

The technical problems of providing public water supplies in developing countries lie more in adapting proven techniques to individual situations than in finding new techniques. Some research is needed into aspects of quality control, including the removal of new pollutants and the role of viruses in the transmission of diseases, but the most pressing need is to discover ways of simplifying the design and construction of plant, of using local skills and materials, and of adapting established procedures so that they can be carried out by a relatively unskilled staff in field conditions. Simplified ways of detecting bacterial and chemical contaminants are also required: a simple go/no-go strip-indicator to tell whether water is adequately chlorinated would be an invention of immeasurable value.

Minor variations in the standard of water purity can be expected from country to country but in general the requirements are universally applicable. Advisory 'International Standards for Drinking Water' are published by the World Health Organisation and periodically revised. They cover the choice of raw water sources; the adequacy of various treatment methods; monitoring, sampling and laboratory testing methods; the maintenance of distribution systems and the production of an 'acceptable' — as distinct from 'safe' — water supply. They are compiled with particular reference to developing countries, incorporate many simplified tests and procedures, and are aimed as much at what is practicably obtainable as at what is ideally desirable. Certain sections, relating to bacteriological, radiological and toxic substances, in respect of which safe limits should never be exceeded, contain rigid recommendations. In other sections, where some flexibility may be permitted according to local circumstances, alternative limits — described as 'highest desirable levels' and 'maximum permissible levels' — are given; the former being a target to achieve wherever practicable.

A separate set of 'European Standards for Drinking Water' contains recommendations more specific to industrialised countries in the temperate zones where the demand is likely to be for water of a higher degree of acceptability — at a correspondingly higher cost — than is required in many tropical countries in their present stages of development. The standards correspond closely in essentials, but in specific detail the European standards depend upon greater availability of laboratory facilities, expertise and ability to undertake sophisticated techniques.

Sewage Disposal

A public water-supply system must be matched by a system of sewers and sewage disposal facilities to remove and purify dirty water, and by a safe means of removing and disposing of solid wastes. Both liquid and solid wastes are growing rapidly in volume and becoming more complex in their make-up, particularly in highly industrialised societies, where the environment is no longer capable of absorbing them and rendering them harmless. Hence a good deal of attention is now being given to the whole process of production and consumption to see how the amount of waste can be reduced.

Wastes concentrate harmful substances and properties which are dangerous to those who handle them and, if they are not disposed of properly, to the general public and the natural environment. The main objectives of waste-disposal systems are: firstly, to confine wastes at their source; secondly, to remove them expeditiously from human surroundings; and thirdly, to treat them, if necessary, to prevent health hazards, nuisances and environmental degradation at the point of disposal.

A tendency to give highest priority to removing wastes from residential areas and to regard the protection of streams, land and communities as a secondary consideration is almost instinctive, but as communities grow, as public demand for pollution control increases and as acceptable disposal sites become scarcer and more distant it becomes imperative to consider waste management in metropolitan areas as a total exercise. Long-term planning and management require the forecasting of future conditions, the formulation and analysis of optional solutions, and the recommendation of courses of action which are technically sound and financially feasible. But planners must at the same time be alert to the fundamental research which is now being undertaken into means of reducing and eliminating waste, for technological breakthroughs could change waste disposal procedures drastically. This should not be regarded as a far-fetched notion, considering that in an age of rapid technological advances there has been little innovation in waste-water treatment for fifty years, and that sewer design has not changed much since the days of Imperial Rome.

In developing countries, however, it remains essential to focus attention on the problems of waste in the home, particularly on the disposal of excreta, which is a vital health factor. In some places toilets are virtually unknown; in others they exist but are not always used. Hence the provision of facilities must be supplemented by health education. In the wider community context more attention must be paid to the health hazards of specific elements in sewage, since a great deal of agricultural land is irrigated with municipal waste water and most large cities draw at least part of their supply from sources into which sewage is discharged. More sensitive indicators for detecting the presence of pathogenic organisms and other contaminants are needed.

There is an urgent need also for basic design data for waste-water systems in developing countries: far too many systems are built without regard to local customs in the use of water and re-use of waste water, or to the available construction methods and materials. Information on existing water supplies, waste-water and storm-water sewerage systems and existing household plumbing is seldom recorded in detail.

Innovation is needed both to produce simple and safe forms of domestic plumbing and sanitary appliances for areas where none exist and to improve the efficiency of existing systems. The possibility of re-using some grades of waste water without treatment — using laundry water to flush toilets, for instance — should be considered. This implies building separate pipe systems for different forms of waste, with safeguards against accidental cross-connections, but it could yield a significant saving in water consumption and permit the use of smaller pipes. More effective treatment systems must be developed to produce a higher standard of effluent and to cope with new contaminants. Existing treatment plants often fail to remove some pollutants and are put out of action by others. This is particularly true where storm water and industrial wastes are mixed with domestic sewage, but even small plants handling only domestic sewage are frequently put out of commission by new chemicals used in the home. The new constituents of sewage must be identified and those which cannot readily be removed by treatment plants should be excluded from the system. Whenever possible new plants should be designed to facilitate experimentation and adaptation to new processes. Automatic monitoring equipment is needed to record discharges and give warning of the presence of dangerous elements. Now that the purification of waste water for human consumption and other uses is becoming technically feasible, more attention must be paid to the health hazards of contaminants and more safeguards against breakdown or faulty operation must be built into treatment plants.

The discharge of raw sewage into fresh water can no longer be tolerated, while discharge into the sea, particularly into estuaries, needs careful control and may have to be restricted. Increasingly, restrictions are being placed on the discharge of industrial wastes into public sewers and watercourses, but such restrictions can cause problems elsewhere — including contamination of groundwater — if firms dump prohibited wastes on land, either within their own sites or on public tips.

It is estimated that only one urban family in eight was served by sewers in developing countries in 1970. The World Health Organisation's target for the Second Development Decade is to raise this ratio to one in three by 1980, which means providing sewers for 180 million people. In developed and developing countries alike the main problem is not technical; it is to persuade people to want and to pay for sewerage schemes. However, public appreciation of the value of proper sanitary facilities is growing.

The authorities concerned must satisfy themselves that adopted schemes are comprehensive — that they take account of all relevant aspects of the problem, including technical, social, economic, political and cultural factors; that they represent the optimum long-term technical solution as far as can be ascertained; and that they are financially sound. Since the objectives of sewage disposal include the promotion of amenities such as health, aesthetic values and recreational opportunities, on which different people place greatly differing values, the method of evaluating benefits is still controversial. Agreed criteria are needed to enable long-term sewerage plans to be given due weight in national economic planning.

Solid Wastes

Solid wastes are a growing problem in developed countries, which now produce some 700 kilogrammes per head per year of domestic refuse and a similar amount of industrial and agricultural wastes. The amounts in developing countries, for which data are lacking, are rapidly catching up. The composition of solid wastes is changing rapidly too, but there is no basis for international comparison since analyses are made for different purposes in different places – to determine either combustibility, compressibility, compostability or the content of reclaimable materials. Recent realisation that solid wastes are 'resources out of place' makes it important to establish uniform classifications, methods of analysis and terminology.

Industrial solid wastes – and liquid wastes which are excluded from municipal sewers and watercourses – need particular attention. A recent study in the United Kingdom[1] concluded that while current disposal practices present few health hazards they would become dangerous in future if not monitored and controlled. Systematic investigation should be carried out in all industrial areas to ascertain how industrial solid wastes are disposed of and to what extent ground and surface waters are or may be contaminated.

The greatest danger to health from domestic refuse often occurs in and around the house, where better methods of handling and storing wastes before collection are needed. In some developing countries tightly-covered refuse bins and refuse chutes have not been notably successful, but plastic sacks appear more promising. In developed countries methods of reducing the amount of refuse before collection need investigating. Burning, grinding, compressing, discharge to the sewers and pneumatic collection have all been tried. The separation of certain wastes, such as paper and metal, may be helpful.

Solid wastes are often processed before dumping to reduce

their volume, stabilise organic compounds, prevent contamination of soil and water, remove toxic or other dangerous elements and recover useful materials. The methods used include grinding, compacting, baling, incineration, pyrolysis and composting. The suitability of these, and possibly other, techniques in the varying circumstances of different countries needs investigating.

With or without treatment, refuse is usually tipped in natural or artificial holes or on low-lying ground. It has, however, been used in some places to make artificial hills for recreational use. Dumping at sea has been practised with some success and it has been suggested that wastes deposited at the edge of the continental shelf would gradually be buried under the ocean floor – an idea which might warrant investigation.

An effective refuse disposal system depends upon good planning, good organisation and community co-operation. Regional disposal schemes should be encouraged, particularly in heavily urbanised areas where tipping sites are scarce. Oganisation is vital to the success of waste-disposal systems and means of improving it should be investigated. One new idea has come from the United States, where one state has set up a 'waste acceptance' agency empowered to make regulations, to accept and dispose of all kinds of waste and to levy charges.

Improvements in water-supply and waste-disposal systems must be accompanied by public education in hygiene, since the intelligent co-operation of the public is vital to the success of such schemes. And it must always be remembered that the objectives are not waterworks but safe water, not sewage works or refuse incinerators but freedom from disease. Large sums of money and the dedicated efforts of many individuals, from the politician to the village pump attendant, will be needed if the problems are to be solved.

9 Transport

Transport Systems

Just as settlements cannot exist without water, they cannot grow and prosper without good communications within their boundaries and with other places. Historically, good communications have been a prime factor governing the location of successful cities, and hardly a single major city or metropolitan region in the world has continued to thrive without good physical links between its own sectors and with the outside world. The world's first megalopolitan region, in the north-eastern United States, is founded on the massive waterway network which nurtured its early industrial development. Similar, if smaller, complexes may be found throughout the world: most primate cities have developed because of their strategic location in relation to trade routes and to other national centres of production and consumption.

As cities grow larger and more diversified in their activities transport between the various sectors becomes more critical and complex, existing systems labour under greater strain and their environmental impact increases. A great volume of movement is imposed upon a pattern of buildings, land uses and streets which evolved when there were fewer people and activities and less movement of people and goods. At the same time current trends in urban growth, including the tendency towards a more dispersed pattern of residential areas – with its associated increase in the use of private motor cars – and the removal of many economic activities from the city centres, have placed strains on existing transport networks and created a need for more efficient systems. In most cities the existing networks have grown piecemeal in response to pressures and crises. The pieces generally do not add up to a system and often preclude the development of one. This has happened particularly in the developed countries but even in the developing world, under the impact of rapid rural-to-urban migration, existing transport networks are coming under acute stress. Most cities have never succeeded completely in solving their transport problems, and their attempts to meet the growing need to move people and goods have an increasingly serious effect on the environment. Whatever their local economic and social characteristics, cities throughout the world in both industrial and transitional economies face similar transport problems.

Because of the amount of space they consume, and of their critical role in linking parts of the city together and enabling it to perform its economic functions, transport systems often determine the overall environment of the city. As urban areas grow and become more crowded the impact of transport systems will be intensified and their demand for space will increase. This means, of course, that there will be less space for other major urban functions — commerce, industry, housing and recreation — and that the quality of urban life is likely to deteriorate. The environmental implications of meeting future transport needs are not yet fully comprehended in most cities. It is extremely doubtful that most cities in both developed and developing countries are adequately prepared for the changes that must take place.

Transport also makes heavy demands on national and municipal budgets. In developing countries in particular the competition for scarce funds between transport, education, housing, water and power supply and other public services is likely to be severe. In consequence these countries tend to invest in transport only when there is a direct economic return in terms of, for instance, lower production costs or increased productivity. Investment tends to follow demand rather than anticipate it and this acts as a check on economic growth. In addition developing countries often attempt to economise by lowering the standards of road construction and maintenance, thereby storing up problems for the future. In the long run the impact of transport on the urban environment can be controlled only by comprehensive land-use/transportation planning, which determines the location of jobs, houses, shops and other urban activities in the light of the traffic flows between them. The careful placing of different land-use activities within the urban area can significantly reduce the amount of movement of people and goods and avoid unnecessary conflicts between traffic flows.

For example, if port and manufacturing activities are located in the same district the distance which many goods have to be carried can be reduced and the movement of goods through residential and central areas can be minimised. Conversely the unco-ordinated growth of various urban functions increases both the need to travel and the conflict between different kinds of traffic moving to different destinations, and at the same time makes it more difficult to provide efficient transport networks.

Thus public control over the shape and size of the city is an important means of reducing environmental conflicts caused by transport systems. This control must apply to both the horizontal and the vertical dimensions of the city. High buildings placed close together increase the density of human and economic activities and thereby concentrate movements, resulting in congestion. Moreover, inadequate capacity for moving goods and people vertically within tall buildings can intensify congestion on the ground. In the Manhattan area of New York studies have shown that out of every hour during which trucks occupy road space, forty-five minutes are spent waiting to deliver goods to buildings. The delays are caused by the inadequate capacity of goods lifts.[2]

The central city core, such as Manhattan, is one of the most critical areas in land-use/transportation planning. The core is the centre of the city's energy and wealth. Vincent Ponte[3] points out that although it covers a relatively small area, the core may produce as much as 20 per cent of the city's taxes. If the core does not function well, the whole city may suffer – and what keeps it from working properly is congestion.

Congestion, Ponte says, is 'mobs of people pouring out of subways and skyscrapers into the streets. It is rows of trucks double-parked at the kerb. Most of all, it is traffic disgorged from the clogged mouth of some freeway now creeping along inch-wise, blocked left and right by walls of pedestrians and pinched into a narrow trickle of double-parked vehicles'. Its impact is 'exhaust fumes, blaring horns, and the racket of trip-hammers and riveters when new skyscrapers will shortly dump thousands into the mêlée. Downtown in our biggest cities is an obstacle course. It is a war of nerves between traffic and pedestrians that is fought out every day almost to a literal standstill.'

Whatever mode of transport is used, people, vehicles and activities will pour into the relatively small area of the city core. If the core is to remain workable without overbearing traffic restrictions, planners must consider the interfaces between people, vehicles and activities. Ponte's solution, which has wide support, is to separate pedestrians, cars, trucks and public transport systems into their own spheres or different physical levels, thus creating for each 'a distinct and appropriate environment where there is easy circulation without mutual interference'. Ponte points out that the idea is not new. For years trains have run on separate levels from other traffic. But now plans are being made for buses to run on elevated expressways into multi-level terminals and for multi-level pedestrian systems extending across city centres to form a lattice connecting transport terminals, car parks and important buildings. The multi-level approach is being applied in Dallas, Texas, where a truck tunnel system will separate goods movement from surface traffic and pedestrians, and in the centres of Montreal and Munich.

In the developed countries, where city centres are already densely packed with people, activities and transport systems, the multi-level approach can be partially applied as a short-term solution but fully applied only in the long term as the city is rebuilt. In developing countries with rapidly growing but still immature cities there is an opportunity to decide now to adopt a multi-level approach. But the decision must be made quickly if the opportunity is not to be swept away by the tidal wave of development.

In the more mature cities of both the developed and the developing world, Ponte says, 'The trend towards multiple block or "super-block" development involving large chunks of downtown real estate is particularly well suited for introducing at one stroke pedestrian, trucking and auto levels in large, self-contained, functioning units that will eventually tie into one another and into the transit systems'. The super-block principle has the added advantage that by concentrating many city functions into a single complex it offers opportunities for maintaining the viability of cities and at the same time reducing the need to travel within the cities.

Other land-use policies, such as the development of new towns or satellite towns, can also contribute to reducing traffic in city centres, but only if the new developments offer employment as well as housing. Similarly the planned re-location of industries and other traffic-generating activities which do not have to be in the city centre can reduce transport conflicts.

If transport systems and urban development are not comprehensively planned, cities face the prospect of a continuous decline in their physical environment and activities, with dangerous consequences for the economic and social well-being of the cities themselves and of the nation as a whole. Transport systems are of critical importance both within the city and between cities and must therefore be planned comprehensively at the national, regional and urban levels. Moreover, since no single mode of transport can meet all needs at the various levels, comprehensive plans must take into account the distribution of traffic between the various modes, the optimal capacity of each mode and the transfer of goods and passengers between modes. It is essential that quantitative analysis of alternative models for regional land-use/transportation strategies should be evolved and used to reveal the interrelationships between the component parts of transport systems and land-use patterns.

The solution to transport and environmental problems at the urban and regional levels lies, therefore, in bringing control of the various sectoral policies and plans into a single co-ordinating organisation. In most cases this organisation will have to be built from scratch. In the more developed countries the problems of institution-building may be compounded by the parochial interests, established rights and prerogatives of existing sectoral institutions. The developing countries may find the institutional problems somewhat easier to solve because they are at an earlier stage of urbanisation.

In some metropolitan areas a form of regional organisation has already been established, but in most cases a more comprehensive organisation is needed in order to achieve real co-ordination. The metropolitan regional planning bodies that have been developed in the United States, for instance, rarely have control over transportation planning and management. In Stockholm, however, one authority is responsible for co-ordinating regional planning, transportation, housing, water supply, sewerage and other activities.

At the national level, particularly in developing countries, governments must evolve a consistent policy for urban transport development. This requires a clear statement of aims as to the types of urban area and urban transport system desired, with clearly designated priorities and a balance between economic development on the one hand and social and environmental considerations on the other. So far most developing countries have made economic development their first priority and they are not likely to allow environmental considerations to deter or divert them from this objective in relation to transport systems. It is important, therefore, that transport and land-use planning should be co-ordinated so that proper regard can be paid to all the relevant issues.

The problems of getting the best out of existing transport networks, the choice between optional modes of transport, and some of the new systems and technologies now under investigation, are examined in more detail in the following sections.

Managing the Motor Car

The problem of the motor car is still, in the main, the problem of the developed countries; but as more countries share in the world's wealth their citizens will increasingly want to own cars. In some parts of the developing world this trend is already apparent. In many Latin American countries, for example, the number of cars for each 1000 inhabitants increased three to four times between 1950 and 1967.[1] In Japan, between 1958 and 1968, the number of cars increased from 226,000 to 5,209,000 — a twenty-threefold increase; and the number of all motor vehicles increased from 700,000 to 12.5 million — an eighteenfold increase.[2]

In the same decade the total number of private and commercial vehicles in the world increased from 112 million to almost 216 million, representing an average annual growth rate of about 4.5 per cent. The sharpest increases were in

Asia, Europe and South America, the smallest in Oceania and North America. But the United States accounted for almost two-thirds of the total number in 1958, and for about half the 1968 total. Europe had about a quarter of the world fleet in 1958, and about one-third in 1968. The average annual growth rate for bus and truck fleets in this period was 6.1 per cent, with the highest rates occurring in the less developed regions, where commercial vehicles represent a far higher proportion of the total fleets than in the developed regions. In 1968 the growth was 32 per cent in Mexico, 55 per cent in Korea and almost 98 per cent in China, against 17 per cent in the U.S.A. and 8.4 per cent in Germany.[3]

The large and growing volume of road traffic in most cities and towns, coupled with the high cost (in terms of investment, space and disruption of existing physical and social structures) of expanding the road network, puts a premium on traffic management schemes designed to make the best use of existing road capacities and to minimise the motor vehicle's environmental impact. To some extent at least the two objectives run together, since effective traffic control which improves the flow of vehicles not only makes conditions more tolerable for the motorist and less expensive for the transport operator, but also reduces the level of pollution (by allowing engines to work more efficiently) and permits the retention of existing street patterns and buildings.

Many new techniques in traffic management are now in operation or under trial as cities respond to the increasing incidence of traffic paralysis. Delft, in the Netherlands, allows buses priority on the streets by devices that actuate traffic lights. Freeways in metropolitan New York, and in many other cities, have metered ramps to control the volume and maintain the flow of traffic. Los Angeles is building a busway; Washington's exclusive bus lane has saved commuters twenty minutes each trip. Chicago has placed rapid-rail tracks and reserved bus lanes in the median strips of three expressways. Computerised traffic-control systems have been installed in many European and North American cities: Toronto's system, covering over 900 intersections, has reduced travel time on an average city-centre trip by 25 per cent. Hamburg, London and Chicago are experimenting with automatic vehicle-monitoring systems which can pinpoint the location of all public service vehicles.

Other schemes have been tried with varying degrees of success in reducing congestion and with varying degrees of opposition from people who have had to change established habits — schemes such as evening goods deliveries, staggered working. hours and night-time goods traffic on underground railways.

As yet, no other form of transport has offered the same degree of personal mobility as the motor car. It is often argued that the sheer number of vehicles and the resulting road congestion in cities, particularly at peak travel times, has reduced this advantage. However, one recent study by Peter C. Koltnow[4] suggests that this is not so: on the contrary, travel time in American cities has improved in recent years as the result of improved road systems, traffic signalling, parking and unloading restrictions, one-way streets and other management measures. Even so, the motor car may have reached or passed the peak of its efficiency as a mode of urban transport. On the freeways of major cities expensive, sophisticated vehicles designed to work efficiently at speeds of 60 to 80 m.p.h. can be seen moving at 10 m.p.h. or less.

Other studies suggest that the delays caused by traffic congestion in cities have become intolerable. The city of Munich, when planning a new rapid-transit system, estimated that its economy was losing almost $27 million a year as a result of the poor traffic conditions.[5] Elsewhere in Germany and in Switzerland, reduced traffic speeds in 1969 resulting from congestion are said to have increased bus operating costs by 1 million DM in Hanover, 1.3 million DM in Dusseldorf, 1.2 million Swiss francs in Zurich and 2.9 million Swiss francs in Basle.[6]

Traffic congestion can be translated into economic costs in terms of lost productive effort, higher vehicle operating costs, increased air pollution and increased accident rates. Although the cost of delays in delivering goods is eventually passed on to consumers, no money figure has ever been attached to it. The economic loss arising from car accidents in the United States of America in 1968 was put at over $10,000 million.

The accidents caused 55,000 deaths and 170,000 permanent disabilities.[7] The emotional costs of delays and hazards on overcrowded roads must also be considered.

The amount of road space needed to move an average of 1.5 persons per car on heavily used routes is excessive both in comparison with other modes of transport and in relation to other urban functions. In central Los Angeles over 60 per cent of the land area is occupied by streets, freeways and parking places. The demands of the motor car are increasingly dictating the layout of urban areas, where the rising ratio of cars to people is inevitably leading authorities to consider to what extent cars can be allowed the freedom of the cities.

Public Transport
The disadvantages of the motor car focus attention on alternative modes of transport, particularly public transport systems. Although the ideal solution lies in a balanced mix of transport modes designed to suit the particular circumstances of each city, many cites are in fact forced to choose between investing in roads and investing in railways and other rapid-transit systems. In the past rail rapid-transit systems have involved higher initial capital costs than highways, but in highly developed urban areas this seems to be no longer true. Urban road construction costs in the United States of America are now ranging from $10 million to $40 million per mile, with higher costs where cuttings and complex interchanges are involved. The estimated construction costs of the San Francisco BART system and the Washington, D.C. METRO are $17.5 million and $30.4 million per mile respectively. In general, the construction costs of rail rapid-transit systems are comparable throughout the world, although related to the specific characteristics of the city and the system involved.

The initial capital costs may be higher in developing countries because much of the hardware has to be imported, while road-building and maintenance costs may be lower because fewer imports are involved and labour is cheap. However, the cost-per-mile yardstick may be irrelevant when set beside land-use and environmental goals. In developing countries, where resources are limited and the prime goal is economic development, the costs of congestion and of air, noise and aesthetic pollution are likely to be less important than in developed countries: a certain level of economic growth is necessary before environmental considerations become apparent. Even so, developing nations should not completely overlook the environmental impact of road transport and the need for a balanced urban transport system. At their present stage of development they may be able to gain advantages, perhaps at little extra cost, by learning from the experiences in transport planning of other nations.

Rapid-transit systems make far less demand on land than roads. The Westinghouse Transit Expressway, a rail system designed for medium-density cities, needs twelve acres per mile for a two-lane track, including stations. A highway of equivalent capacity would need fourteen lanes taking up 100 acres per mile. The capacity of rail systems ranges from 30,000 to 60,000 passengers an hour on one track. One highway lane can carry 2000 cars an hour, which, at an average of 1.5 persons per car, gives a capacity of 3000 passengers an hour.[8]

In many developed cities a calculated acceptance of a tolerable degree of road congestion may be a necessary element in transport planning. However, there can be little doubt that in many parts of the world a major emphasis is being placed oń providing improved public transport. The balance between public and private transport is one of the most critical areas of decision in long-range planning. Where private transport has become over-dominant, public transport must be made sufficiently attractive and responsive to individual needs to woo people away from their cars.

It has been pointed out that 'in Europe, good public transportation is a tradition, in the United States it is an argument'.[9] Europeans think in terms of moving people and goods − not cars − and the importance of good public transport, particularly railway systems, is well understood. Munich's underground railway has been designed specifically to play an important part in preserving the city's character − to have 'an important bearing upon urban policy, urban planning and the urban economy'. Its proponents argued 'from the aspect of urban planning, the rails of a rapid-transit system must be regarded as the skeleton preventing the dissolution of the city in the surrounding country. The possibility of fast and easy traffic from the environs to the city centre, or from one part of the city to another, opens up a number of possibilities for creating within the reach of a mass transportation system self-contained sub-centres.'[10]

Transport Planning

It has been suggested that in spite of all the potential inherent advantages of rapid-transit railways, most of the actual benefits occur as unplanned side-effects. There are a number of reasons for this deficiency in planning. One is that the rapid-transit industry has confined itself to limited goals concerned primarily with seeking out lucrative concentrations of journey-to-work passengers. This was a profitable method of operation before the advent of widespread car ownership but it is not the right goal in the face of rising competition from the motor car. In many cases the result of continuing preoccupation with this goal has been rising operating deficits. But in spite of the emphasis placed on fare revenues as the basis of decision-making, many public transport systems, particularly in the United States of America, are increasingly dependent on subsidies — and the extent of the subsidy is determining the planning policies of the operators. But planning on the basis of a minimum subsidy does not provide for the real needs of urban areas. An alternative approach was outlined by William H. Liskam at the Fourth International Conference on Urban Transportation in March 1969. Liskam said, 'Only when our transportation systems are planned to include potential social, economic, environmental and other community benefits, and receive financial priority appropriate to these benefits, will these systems begin to realise their full potential as major contributors to the successful functioning of the community'.[11]

However, institutional difficulties lie in the path of such an approach to transport planning. Most of the existing rapid-transit organisations are not equipped to deal with the broader issues of public transport policy. In most cities the rapid-transit agency is separate from the body or bodies responsible for road construction, parking policy, development control, road transport and social programmes. In many places rapid-transit railways and road passenger services compete on the same routes, to the disadvantage of everyone. Moreover, many transit systems extend beyond the administrative boundaries of the city into communities which are outside the city's jurisdiction and tax base. The desired co-ordination between competing modes of transport, between autónomous authorities and agencies and between public and private interests requires a major organisational effort.

The total system for moving goods and people in the city must involve more than roads and railways: lifts, escalators, footpaths and moving pavements may be needed to complete the linkages. In Europe there are a good many examples of such multi-mode transport systems, particularly in the Federal Republic of Germany, Sweden, Hungary and the Union of Soviet Socialist Republics. Without the necessary linkages, an increased volume of traffic on any one mode invariably causes a rippling or congesting effect on the adjacent sectors of the system. It is at the interfaces between transport modes that co-ordination can be most difficult. For example, the effects of increased air travel have not yet been efficiently absorbed by other modes of transport.

New Technologies
Technological advances in a number of fields hold out the promise of solving or reducing some transport problems. The direct solution to air pollution from transport, for instance, lies in the development of non-polluting engines, and most motor manufacturers are now conducting research on these lines. In the meantime efforts can be and are being made to reduce noxious emissions by regulations involving the modification of engines and the control of the use of vehicles. Pricing mechanisms are another possible means of tackling the problem. It is still debatable, however, whether people in developed or developing countries are willing to bear the costs of such controls.

Some of the newly installed or extended rapid-transit systems incorporate advances in vehicle design and vehicle and passenger control. A number of new systems are under investigation. In the field of rapid transit these include monorail systems, dual road-rail vehicles, busways and tracked air-cushion vehicles. An even larger number of systems are being considered for carrying people and goods within city centres and other complexes. Many of these involve continuously moving vehicles or belts, or automatic guidance systems. Needless to say, if these systems become operational they will have an impact on the total transport system and on the environment. If we accept that misuse of technology has created many of the current environmental problems of our towns, we must insist that the potential impact of these new systems be critically studied before they are installed.

Techniques for reducing traffic noise are still in their infancy, since awareness of the potential harmfulness of noise is relatively recent. Some noise-reduction features have been embodied in road design, such as the use of fine-grained, skid-resistant asphalt surfaces which transmit less noise; putting roads through built-up areas into cuttings; and planting trees and shrubs as noise barriers. The first and second examples are effective although costly, but the benefits of the third are not very substantial. Other possibilities lie in the redesigning of motor vehicles. Probably there are greater potential gains to be had from land-use planning and restriction of the use of noisy vehicles in 'quiet zones'. More needs to be known about the way sound flows over the varied profiles of townscapes. It is well known that high-rise buildings on narrow streets intensify traffic noise and contribute to the constant traffic roar that is experienced in cities like New York, but research is needed to see if relatively inexpensive modifications of the urban structure can reduce noise levels.

The notion that improved telecommunications will reduce the demand for transportation is probably a myth. It is quite obvious that the telephone, teleprinter and other communication systems have replaced some of the travel needed to complete business transactions and to report and analyse political and economic developments. But historical trends have clearly indicated that when communications improve, the flow of commerce, ideas, technical information and cultural exchange increases — in other words the movement of both people and goods is stimulated. It is difficult, therefore, to see how closed-circuit television or any other new development in the near future can produce a different result, or how electronic communications can replace face-to-face contacts and interactions.

A greater international exchange of information and experience and joint ventures in research and development would prevent costly duplication of effort. The wider spread of information on technical aspects and, more particularly, organisational aspects of transport systems would help developing nations, which also stand in need of technical assistance. The development of international standards in transportation and related environmental fields would be a worth-while task.

10 Social and Cultural Aspects

The Symbolic Role of the City Centre
The city centre plays a key role in the social and cultural life
of a community. It very largely determines, in the eyes of the
inhabitants and of visitors and tourists, the social, political
and aesthetic prestige of the city. This is true of any city, but
the importance and sphere of influence of the central area is
correspondingly greater and wider in the case of capital cities
and great metropolitan areas. Here the centre is a symbol of
national culture and character, and it plays a decisive role in
creating the 'myth' of the capital city. We can see this
demonstrated in the way airline posters represent New York
by Manhattan, Moscow by Red Square and Paris by the
Champs Élysées.

The central area usually contains a great concentration of
important public buildings, memorial statues and monuments
and other symbols of the collective memory and heritage of
the people. It is the place of ceremonial processions, public
celebrations and political demonstrations. The importance
people attach to the established form and character of the
central area of a capital city is demonstrated by the
reconstruction of the historic Old Town and Royal Tract of
Warsaw after its devastation during World War II. This was a
common effort of the whole nation which has won the
approval both of the Polish people and of tourists. More
recently, the Old Town of Skopje in Yugoslavia was similarly
reconstructed after the city had been ruined by an earth-
quake.

Interactions and Conflicts
The centre of most large cities contains a great diversity of
activities: government, business, finance, industry, shopping,
tourism, culture, entertainment and housing, all closely

packed and intermingled within a relatively small area. The centre of Warsaw, which occupies only about 4.5 per cent of the area of the city, has 35.7 per cent of its jobs, including 76 per cent of those in public administration, 90 per cent of those in finance and insurance, 59 per cent of those in shops, stores and commerce, and 47 per cent of those in scientific, educational and cultural establishments. It has 84 per cent of the city's administrative offices, 87 per cent of its theatres, 75 per cent of its museums, all its concert halls, 85 per cent of its hotels, 65 per cent of its restaurants and cafés and 44 per cent of its shops and stores. Journeys to the central area account for 51.5 per cent of all passengers carried by public transport and 75 per cent of all vehicular traffic.

It is this concentration and diversity of interacting functions that makes the centre such an exciting, vital and important place, but at the same time it gives rise to a number of damaging conflicts. Some of these arise from the presence of activities which are not compatible with the central area, either because — like some industries — they are detrimental to its environment or because — as in the case of hospitals — the busy and noisy central area does not provide a suitable environment for the activity concerned. Central areas are characterised by facilities serving the whole city or an even wider sphere, but not all facilities which have this purpose are suited to the central area. Large scientific institutions, higher-education establishments and large sports centres are among those which are better dispersed to other locations.

The activities appropriate to the central area are those whose success depends upon their concentration in close proximity to one another. All of them are activities that must be easily accessible to large numbers of people. But these two characteristics — concentration and accessibility — give rise to a second kind of conflict — when, for example, a railway station or multi-storey car park is placed next to a museum, theatre or residential block. Conflicts between vehicle and pedestrian circulation systems fall into this category too, as do conflicts caused by the juxtaposition of traffic-generating activities, particularly when they produce simultaneous peak-hour concentrations of people and vehicles. This sort of conflict can be avoided only by good urban planning, the aim of which should be not only to separate conflicting activities, but also to juxtapose those which mutually benefit from proximity and to locate all activities in relation to transport facilities in accordance with the demands they make on the transport system.

In particular, easy access on foot to all central-area facilities is essential to the proper working of the centre both as a focus of intensive and varied activities and as a forum for social and cultural interchange and integration. This is why the central area must be compact and why vehicular and pedestrian circulation systems should be physically separated.

Increasingly, the traditional city-centre pattern of individual buildings occupying separate plots and facing on to streets is being replaced by large multi-functional complexes of interrelated structures. Developments of this kind can yield great social, economic and spatial benefits, but they require careful co-ordination of design, investment and construction activities, including the provision of public utilities and infrastructures. Design co-ordination should extend to the details of street furniture — telephone kiosks, news-stands, benches, posters and illuminated signs — which can enhance the spatial composition of buildings and open areas but can just as easily spoil it. But even the most meticulous central-area plan should allow for spontaneous, unplanned activities, for these too are of the essence of city centres. Such characteristic features as the soap-box orators at Hyde Park Corner in London, the second-hand booksellers along the Seine in Paris, and the exhibition of paintings on the fortifications of the Old Town in Warsaw, enrich the atmosphere of the city.

The rapid march of science and technology makes it impossible to forecast the long-term material and cultural needs of urban areas, particularly those of central areas, which are the first to reflect the newest trends. It is essential, therefore, that the central-area plan should be as flexible as possible. Room should be left for the introduction of new functions by the replacement of obsolete buildings or by more radical redevelopment. Similarly, buildings should be capable of adaptation to new needs: they should be structures in which the internal space can easily be re-arranged.

Historic Areas

The centres of long-established cities usually contain areas of considerable antiquity which contribute to their unique character and importance but at the same time often conflict with the bustling activities of a modern national or regional capital. These historic quarters often occupy some of the most valuable land, hinder the introduction of new activities and obstruct the building of new roads and public transport systems. Their buildings may be in bad repair and unsuited to modern needs and demands. Such areas often contain some of the worst housing conditions in the city. Nevertheless their aesthetic, historic and cultural significance is one of the main tourist attractions of many cities, and thereby constitutes an important source of state and municipal income.

In many cities this architectural and cultural heritage is constantly threatened by the expansion of city-centre activities and the consequent demand for new buildings, which in design and scale are often out of sympathy with the remnants of the past and indistinguishable from those of other cities around the world. Historic areas should be treated as valuable artefacts: they need the sort of care and expertise that are found in museums and art galleries. But they should not be frozen. 'Open-air museums' which preserve the ancient fabric and atmosphere intact have a historical and educational value of their own, but the purpose of the central-area plan should be to integrate the older parts into the modern city. New buildings can be fitted into the old quarter provided their design is in harmony with their surroundings, and old buildings can be converted to new uses and provided with modern amenities. It may be necessary to prohibit the erection of tall or massive buildings within, or on the fringes of, such areas, but it should be remembered that the sympathetic juxtaposition of the old and the new can produce exhilarating new townscapes.

The conservation and rehabilitation of historic areas and their integration into the life and structure of the modern city centre present planners and administrators with problems of considerable intricacy which cannot always be solved by conventional techniques or within the framework of existing organisations. But the difficulties are not insuperable. Vienna within the Ringstrasse, Le Marais in Paris and the Vieux Carré in New Orleans are excellent examples of how historic quarters can be rehabilitated in such a way that they remain a link with the past yet contribute to the modern life of the city. In these areas old buildings have been refurbished, sub-standard houses have been either improved or demolished and structures have been adapted to new uses, resulting in an 'urban mix' that is satisfying and stimulating.

In many countries individual historic buildings and monuments are listed and protected by law, their architectural and structural features are recorded and their fabric is restored. All too often, however, other buildings nearby which form part of the same townscape have been replaced by modern ones, breaking both the visual and the historic continuity. Detailed inventories are seldom made of groups of buildings and whole districts, though detailed knowledge of the characteristics, structural condition and present role of the buildings is needed as the basis of conservation planning. There is, however, a growing appreciation of the value of preserving groups of buildings rather than isolated ones.

The UNESCO General Conference of 1968 adopted international 'Recommendations Concerning the Preservation of Cultural Properties Endangered by Public and Private Works' which stressed the need for a thorough survey of historic quarters. Such surveys should record the physical features and the socio-economic situation of the area concerned. Aerial and ground-level photography can be used to record the layout and form of buildings and streets. In some countries architectural details are coded and stored in computers; in some architectural photogrammetry — a technique involving accurate stereo-photographs from which line drawings can be made — is used to complete the records.

Once inventories are completed, areas can be designated for conservation and plans prepared for long-term restoration and improvement programmes. Activities which are not appropriate to the area should be transferred to suitable alternative locations. If an area is in a state of decay, the former facilities and character of the site should be restored as soon as possible and brought up to modern standards of comfort and hygiene; shop premises should be modernised or new shops carefully incorporated in existing buildings; and businesses which meet local needs or attract tourists — such as jewellers and antique dealers — should be encouraged. Regulations will be needed to prevent the demolition and control the restoration or alteration of existing buildings and to govern the design of new buildings. Normal building regulations may have to be amended to meet the special circumstances of conservation areas. Commercial advertising by means of posters and illuminated signs should be strictly limited and controlled. The regulations should be supported by penalties for non-observance and by the provision of technical advice, grants and low-interest loans to help residents and small businesses to carry out restoration schemes. In addition historic buildings may be exempted from local taxes to offset the combined effect of high land values and non-profit-making or low-profitability activities. Conservation schemes and compatible developments can be stimulated by the award of certificates, plaques and medals.

Citizenship and Participation

Central areas provide people with unique opportunities for meeting each other and reinforcing their sense of belonging to the wider community of the city. The personal sense of belonging to a separate local community, class or other group is lost in the anonymity of the city, while the multiplicity of activities enables people from different backgrounds to join together in the pursuit of common interests in which their differences are minimised. But the same sense of anonymity and escape from the control of public opinion and traditions helps to create egotistic and anti-social attitudes, and even facilitates social disorganisation and criminal activity. One effect of this lack of social constraint is found in the evolution of a separate teenage culture, whose progressive features are counterbalanced by ills ranging from the harmless extravagances of youth to delinquency and sexual perversion.

The social values of the central area are a function of the emotional ties of the inhabitants to their city — their interest in its past, present and future, their feeling of joint responsibility for its fate. Such feelings must be fostered by public participation in the planning and management of the city. Participation depends upon a good flow of information and public debate on official actions and intentions, plans and policies; a process in which public institutions, professional bodies, voluntary societies and the communications media all play an important part.

Appendix

INTRODUCTORY REMARKS

The Conference adopted a Declaration on the Human Environment and an Action Plan containing 109 recommendations for all sectors. The text of the Declaration and the recommendations concerning human settlements are given below.

The General Assembly of the United Nations, at its twenty-seventh session (September–December 1972), considered the report on the proceedings of the Conference and adopted several resolutions concerning this subject. The main resolution establishes a Governing Council for Environmental Programmes and a co-ordinating Board, the Environment Secretariat and an Environment Fund, whose functions are outlined in the resolution reproduced below. The Assembly also established the Environment Secretariat in Nairobi, Kenya. The General Assembly adopted three resolutions specifically dealing with Human Settlements, which are also given here.

DECLARATION ON THE HUMAN ENVIRONMENT

The United Nations Conference on the Human Environment,
Having met at Stockholm from 5 to 16 June 1972,
Having considered the need for a common outlook and for common principles to inspire and guide the peoples of the world in the preservation and enhancement of the human environment,

I

Proclaims that:

1. Man is both creature and moulder of his environment, which gives him physical sustenance and affords him the opportunity for intellectual, moral, social and spiritual growth. In the long and tortuous evolution of the human race on this planet a stage has been reached when, through the rapid acceleration of science and technology, man has acquired the power to transform his environment in countless ways and on an unprecedented scale. Both aspects of man's environment, the natural and the man-made, are essential to his well-being and to the enjoyment of basic human rights — even the right to life itself.

2. The protection and improvement of the human environment is a major issue which affects the well-being of peoples and economic development throughout the world; it is the urgent desire of the peoples of the whole world and the duty of all Governments.

3. Man has constantly to sum up experience and go on discovering, inventing, creating and advancing. In our time, man's capability to transform his surroundings, if used wisely, can bring to all peoples the benefits of development and the opportunity to enhance the quality of life. Wrongly or heedlessly applied, the same power can do incalculable harm to human beings and the human environment. We see around us growing evidence of man-made harm in many regions of the earth: dangerous levels of pollution in water, air, earth and living beings; major and undesirable disturbances to the ecological balance of the biosphere; destruction

and depletion of irreplaceable resources; and gross deficiencies harmful to the physical, mental and social health of man, in the man-made environment, particularly in the living and working environment.

4. In the developing countries most of the environmental problems are caused by underdevelopment. Millions continue to live far below the minimum levels required for a decent human existence, deprived of adequate food and clothing, shelter and education, health and sanitation. Therefore, the developing countries must direct their efforts to development, bearing in mind their priorities and the need to safeguard and improve the environment. For the same purpose, the industralised countries should make efforts to reduce the gap between themselves and the developing countries. In the industrialised countries, environmental problems are generally related to industrialisation and technological development.

5. The natural growth of population continuously presents problems on the preservation of the environment, and adequate policies and measures should be adopted, as appropriate, to face these problems. Of all things in the world, people are the most precious. It is the people that propel social progress, create social wealth, develop science and technology and, through their hard work, continuously transform the human environment. Along with social progress and the advance of production, science and technology, the capability of man to improve the environment increases with each passing day.

6. A point has been reached in history when we must shape our actions throughout the world with a more prudent care for their environmental consequences. Through ignorance or indifference we can do massive and irreversible harm to the earthly environment on which our life and well-being depend. Conversely, through fuller knowledge and wiser action, we can achieve for ourselves and our posterity a better life in an environment more in keeping with human needs and hopes. There are broad vistas for the enhancement of environmental quality and the creation of a good life. What is needed is an enthusiastic but calm state of mind and intense but orderly work. For the purpose of attaining

freedom in the world of nature, man must use knowledge to build, in collaboration with nature, a better environment. To defend and improve the human environment for present and future generations has become an imperative goal for mankind — a goal to be pursued together with, and in harmony with, the established and fundamental goals of peace and of world-wide economic and social development.

7. To achieve this environmental goal will demand the acceptance of responsibility by citizens and communities and by enterprises and institutions at every level, all sharing equitably in common efforts. Individuals in all walks of life as well as organisations in many fields, by their values and the sum of their actions, will shape the world environment of the future. Local and national governments will bear the greatest burden for large-scale environmental policy and action within their jurisdictions. International co-operation is also needed in order to raise resources to support the developing countries in carrying out their responsibilities in this field. A growing class of environmental problems, because they are regional or global in extent or because they affect the common international realm, will require extensive co-operation among nations and action by international organizations in the common interest. The Conference calls upon Governments and peoples to exert common efforts for the preservation and improvement of the human environment, for the benefit of all the people and for their posterity.

II

States the common conviction that:

Principle 1
Man has the fundamental right to freedom, equality and adequate conditions of life, in an environment of a quality that permits a life of dignity and well-being, and he bears a solemn responsibility to protect and improve the environment for present and future generations. In this respect, policies promoting or perpetuating *apartheid*, racial segregation, discrimination, colonial and other forms of oppression

and foreign domination stand condemned and must be eliminated.

Principle 2
The natural resources of the earth including the air, water, land, flora and fauna and especially representative samples of natural ecosystems must be safeguarded for the benefit of present and future generations through careful planning or management, as appropriate.

Principle 3
The capacity of the earth to produce vital renewable resources must be maintained and, wherever practicable, restored or improved.

Principle 4
Man has a special responsibility to safeguard and wisely manage the heritage of wildlife and its habitat which are now gravely imperilled by a combination of adverse factors. Nature conservation including wildlife must therefore receive importance in planning for economic development.

Principle 5
The non-renewable resources of the earth must be employed in such a way as to guard against the danger of their future exhaustion and to ensure that benefits from such employment are shared by all mankind.

Principle 6
The discharge of toxic substances or of other substances and the release of heat, in such quantities or concentrations as to exceed the capacity of the environment to render them harmless, must be halted in order to ensure that serious or irreversible damage is not inflicted upon ecosystems. The just struggle of the peoples of all countries against pollution should be supported.

Principle 7
States shall take all possible steps to prevent pollution of the seas by substances that are liable to create hazards to human

health, to harm living resources and marine life, to damage amenities or to interfere with other legitimate uses of the sea.

Principle 8
Economic and social development is essential for ensuring a favourable living and working environment for man and for creating conditions on earth that are necessary for the improvement of the quality of life.

Principle 9
Environmental deficiencies generated by the conditions of underdevelopment and natural disasters pose grave problems and can best be remedied by accelerated development through the transfer of substantial quantities of financial and technological assistance as a supplement to the domestic effort of the developing countries and such timely assistance as may be required.

Principle 10
For the developing countries, stability of prices and adequate earnings for primary commodities and raw material are essential to environmental management since economic factors as well as ecological processes must be taken into account.

Principle 11
The environmental policies of all States should enhance and not adversely affect the present or future development potential of developing countries, nor should they hamper the attainment of better living conditions for all, and appropriate steps should be taken by States and international organisations with a view to reaching agreement on meeting the possible national and international economic con-sequences resulting from the application of environmental measures.

Principle 12
Resources should be made available to preserve and improve the environment, taking into account the circumstances and particular requirements of developing countries and any costs which may emanate from their incorporating environmental

safeguards into their development planning and the need for making available to them, upon their request, additional international technical and financial assistance for this purpose.

Principle 13
In order to achieve a more rational management of resources and thus to improve the environment, States should adopt an integrated and co-ordinated approach to their development planning so as to ensure that development is compatible with the need to protect and improve the human environment for the benefit of their population.

Principle 14
Rational planning constitutes an essential tool for reconciling any conflict between the needs of development and the need to protect and improve the environment.

Principle 15
Planning must be applied to human settlements and urbanisation with a view to avoiding adverse effects on the environment and obtaining maximum social, economic and environmental benefits for all. In this respect projects which are designed for colonialist and racist domination must be abandoned.

Principle 16
Demographic policies, which are without prejudice to basic human rights and which are deemed appropriate by Governments concerned, should be applied in those regions where the rate of population growth or excessive population concentrations are likely to have adverse effects on the environment or development, or where low population density may prevent improvement of the human environment and impede development.

Principle 17
Appropriate national institutions must be entrusted with the task of planning, managing or controlling the environmental resources of States with the view to enhancing environmental quality.

Principle 18
Science and technology, as part of their contribution to economic and social development, must be applied to the identification, avoidance and control of environmental risks and the solution of environmental problems and for the common good of mankind.

Principle 19
Education in environmental matters, for the younger generation as well as adults, giving due consideration to the underprivileged, is essential in order to broaden the basis for an enlightened opinion and responsible conduct by individuals, enterprises and communities in protecting and improving the environment in its full human dimension. It is also essential that mass media of communications avoid contributing to the deterioration of the environment, but, on the contrary, disseminate information of an educational nature, on the need to protect and improve the environment in order to enable man to develop in every respect.

Principle 20
Scientific research and development in the context of environmental problems, both national and multinational, must be promoted in all countries, especially the developing countries. In this connexion, the free flow of up-to-date scientific information and transfer of experience must be supported and assisted, to facilitate the solution of environmental problems; environmental technologies should be made available to developing countries on terms which would encourage their wide dissemination without constituting an economic burden on the developing countries.

Principle 21
States have, in accordance with the Charter of the United Nations and the principles of international law, the sovereign right to exploit their own resources pursuant to their own environmental policies, and the responsibility to ensure that activities within their jurisdiction or control do not cause damage to the environment of other States or of areas beyond the limits of national jurisdiction.

Principle 22
States shall co-operate to develop further the international law regarding liability and compensation for the victims of pollution and other environmental damage caused by activities within the jurisdiction or control of such States to areas beyond their jurisdiction.

Principle 23
Without prejudice to such criteria as may be agreed upon by the international community, or to standards which will have to be determined nationally, it will be essential in all cases to consider the systems of values prevailing in each country, and the extent of the applicability of standards which are valid for the most advanced countries but which may be inappropriate and of unwarranted social cost for the developing countries.

Principle 24
International matters concerning the protection and improvement of the environment should be handled in a co-operative spirit by all countries, big or small, on an equal footing. Co-operation through multilateral or bilateral arrangements or other appropriate means is essential to effectively control, prevent, reduce and eliminate adverse environmental effects resulting from activities conducted in all spheres, in such a way that due account is taken of the sovereignty and interests of all States.

Principle 25
States shall ensure that international organisations play a co-ordinated, efficient and dynamic role for the protection and improvement of the environment.

Principle 26
Man and his environment must be spared the effects of nuclear weapons and all other means of mass destruction. States must strive to reach prompt agreement, in the relevant international organs, on the elimination and complete destruction of such weapons.

RECOMMENDATIONS OF THE UNITED NATIONS CONFERENCE ON THE HUMAN ENVIRONMENT CONCFRNING HUMAN SETTLEMENTS

Recommendation 1

The planning, improvement and management of rural and urban settlements demand an approach, at all levels, which embraces all aspects of the human environment, both natural and man-made. Accordingly, **it is recommended**:

(*a*) *That all development assistance agencies*, whether *international*, such as the United Nations Development Programme and the International Bank for Reconstruction and Development, *regional* or *national*, should in their development assistance activities also give *high priority* within available resources to requests from Governments for assistance in the planning of *human settlements*, notably in housing, transportation, water, sewerage and public health, the mobilisation of human and financial resources, the improvement of transitional urban settlements and the provision and maintenance of essential community services, in order to achieve as far as possible the social well-being of the receiving country as a whole;

(*b*) That these agencies also be prepared to assist the less industrialised countries in solving the environmental problems of development projects; to this end they should actively support the training and encourage the recruitment of requisite personnel, as far as possible within these countries themselves.

Recommendation 2

1. **It is recommended** that *Governments* should designate to the Secretary-General *areas in which they have committed themselves* (or are prepared to commit themselves) to a long-term programme of improvement and global promotion of the environment.

(*a*) In this connexion, countries are invited *to share internationally all relevant information* on the problems they encounter and the solutions they devise in developing these areas.

(*b*) Countries concerned will presumably *appoint an*

appropriate body to plan such a programme, and to supervise its implementation, for areas which could vary in size from a city block to a national region; presumably, too, the programme will be designated to serve, among other purposes, as a vehicle for the preparation and launching of experimental and *pilot projects.*

(*c*) Countries which are willing to launch an improvement programme should be prepared to welcome *international co-operation*, seeking the *advice or assistance of competent international bodies.*

2. It is further recommended:

(*a*) That in order to ensure the success of the programme, Governments should urge the Secretary-General *to undertake a process of planning and co-ordination* whereby contact would be established with nations likely to participate in the programme; *international teams of experts might be assembled for that purpose;*

(*b*) *That a Conference/Demonstration on Experimental Human Settlements* should be held under the auspices of the United Nations in order to provide for co-ordination and the exchange of information and to demonstrate to world public opinion the potential of this approach by means of a display of experimental projects;

(*c*) That nations should take into consideration Canada's offer to organise such Conference/Demonstration and to act as host to it.

Recommendation 3
Certain aspects of human settlements can have international implications, for example, the 'export' of pollution from urban and industrial areas, and the effects of seaports on international hinterlands. Accordingly, **it is recommended** that the attention of Governments be drawn to the need to consult bilaterally or regionally whenever environmental conditions or development plans in one country could have repercussions in one or more neighbouring countries.

Recommendation 4
1. It is recommended that Governments and the Secretary-General, the latter in consultation with the appropriate

United Nations agencies, take the following steps:

(*a*) Entrust the overall responsibility for an agreed programme of environmental research at the international level to any *central body that may be given the co-ordinating authority* in the field of the environment, taking into account the co-ordination work already being provided on the regional level, especially by the Economic Commission for Europe;

(*b*) Identify, wherever possible, an existing agency within the United Nations system as *the principal focal point for initiating and co-ordinating research* in each principal area and, where there are competing claims, establish appropriate priorities;

(*c*) Designate the following as priority areas for research:

   (i) Theories, policies and methods for the comprehensive environmental development of urban and rural settlements;

  (ii) Methods of assessing quantitative *housing needs* and of formulating and implementing phased programmes designed to satisfy them (principal bodies responsible: Department of Economic and Social Affairs of the United Nations Secretariat, regional economic commissions and United Nations Economic and Social Office in Beirut);

  (iii) *Environmental socio-economic indicators* of the quality of human settlements, particularly in terms of desirable occupancy standards and residential densities, with a view to identifying their time trends;

  (iv) *Socio-economic and demographic factors* underlying migration and spatial distribution of population, including the problem of transitional settlements (principal bodies responsible: Department of Economic and Social Affairs of the United Nations Secretariat [Centre for Housing, Building and Planning], United Nations Educational, Scientific and Cultural Organisation, World Health Organisation, International Labour Organisation, Food and Agriculture Organisation of the United Nations);

  (v) *Designs, technologies, financial and administrative procedures* for the efficient and expanded production *of housing* and related infrastructure, suitably adapted to local conditions;

(vi) *Water supply, sewerage and waste-disposal systems* adapted to local conditions, particularly in semi-tropical, tropical, Arctic and sub-Arctic area (principal body responsible: World Health Organisation);

(vii) Alternative methods of meeting rapidly increasing *urban transportation needs* (principal bodies responsible: Department of Economic and Social Affairs of the United Nations Secretariat [Resources and Transport Division and Centre for Housing, Building and Planning]);

(viii) Physical, mental and social effects of *stresses created by living and working conditions in human settlements*, particularly urban conglomerates, for example the accessibility of buildings to persons whose physical mobility is impaired (principal bodies responsible: International Labour Organisation, World Health Organisation, United Nations Educational, Scientific and Cultural Organisation, Department of Economic and Social Affairs of the United Nations Secretariat).

2. **It is further recommended** that Governments consider co-operative arrangements to undertake the necessary research whenever the above-mentioned problem areas have a specific regional impact. In such cases, provision should be made for the *exchange of information and research* findings with countries of other geographical regions sharing similar problems.

Recommendation 5

It is recommended:

(*a*) That Governments take steps to arrange for the exchange of visits by those who are conducting research in the public or private institutions of their countries;

(*b*) That Governments and the Secretary-General ensure the acceleration of the *exchange of information* concerning past and on-going research, experimentation and project implementation covering all aspects of human settlements, which is conducted by the United Nations system or by public or private entities including academic institutions.

Recommendation 6
It is recommended that Governments and the Secretary-General give urgent attention to the *training* of those who are needed to promote integrated action on the planning, development and management of human settlements.

Recommendation 7
It is recommended:
(*a*) That Governments and the Secretary-General provide *equal possibilities for everybody*, both by training and by ensuring access to relevant means and information, to influence their own environment by themselves;
(*b*) That Governments and the Secretary-General ensure that *the institutions concerned shall be strengthened* and that special training activities shall be established, making use of existing projects of regional environmental development, for the benefit of the less industrialised countries, covering the following:
  (i) Intermediate and auxiliary personnel for national public services who, in turn, would be in a position to train others for similar tasks (principal bodies responsible: World Health Organization, Department of Economic and Social Affairs of the United Nations Secretariat [Centre for Housing, Building and Planning], United Nations Industrial Development Organisation, Food and Agriculture Organisation of the United Nations);
 (ii) Specialists in environmental planning and in rural development (principal bodies responsible: Department of Economic and Social Affairs of the United Nations Secretariat [Centre for Housing, Building and Planning], Food and Agriculture Organisation of the United Nations);
(iii) Community developers for self-help programmes for low-income groups (principal body responsible: Department of Economic and Social Affairs of the United Nations Secretariat [Centre for Housing, Building and Planning]);

(iv) Specialists in working conditions (principal bodies responsible: International Labour Organisation, Department of Economic and Social Affairs of the United Nations Secretariat [Centre for Housing, Building and Planning], World Health Organisation);

(v) Planners and organisers of mass transport systems and services, with special reference to environmental development (principal body responsible: Department of Economic and Social Affairs of the United Nations Secretariat [Resources and Transport Division]).

Recommendation 8

It is recommended that regional institutions take stock of the requirements of their regions for various environmental skills and of the facilities available to meet those requirements in order to facilitate the provision of appropriate training within regions.

Recommendation 9

It is recommended that the World Health Organisation increase its efforts to support Governments in planning for improving water supply and sewerage services through its community water supply programme, taking account, as far as possible, of the framework of total environment programmes for communities.

Recommendation 10

It is recommended that development assistance agencies should give higher priority, where justified in the light of the social benefits, to supporting Governments in financing and setting up services for water supply, disposal of water from all sources, and liquid-waste and solid-waste disposal and treatment as part of the objectives of the Second United Nations Development Decade.

Recommendation 11

It is recommended that the Secretary-General ensure that during the preparations for the 1974 World Population Conference, special attention shall be given to population concerns as they relate to the environment and, more particularly, to the environment of human settlements.

Recommendation 12

1. **It is recommended** that the World Health Organisation and other United Nations agencies should provide increased assistance to Governments which so request in the field of family planning programmes without delay.

2. **It is further recommended** that the World Health Organisation should promote and intensify research endeavour in the field of human reproduction, so that the serious consequences of population explosion on human environment can be prevented.

Recommendation 13

It is recommended that the United Nations agencies should focus special attention on the provision of assistance for combating the menace of human malnutrition rampant in many parts of the world. Such assistance will cover training, research and development endeavours on such matters as causes of malnutrition, mass production of high-protein and multipurpose foods, qualitative and quantitative characteristics of routine foods, and the launching of applied nutrition programmes.

Recommendation 14

It is recommended that the *intergovernmental body for environmental affairs to be established within the United Nations* should ensure that the required surveys shall be made concerning the need and the technical possibilities for developing internationally agreed standards and measuring and limiting noise emissions and that, if it is deemed advisable, such standards shall be applied in the production of means of transportation and certain kinds of working equipment, without a large price increase or reduction in the aid given to developing countries.

Recommendation 15

It is recommended that the Secretary-General, in consultation with the appropriate United Nations bodies, *formulate programmes on a world-wide basis to assist countries to meet effectively the requirements of growth of human settlements and to improve the quality of life in existing settlements*; in particular, *in squatter areas.*

Recommendation 16

The programmes referred to in Recommendation 15 should include *the establishment of subregional centres* to undertake, *inter alia*, the following functions:

(*a*) Training;
(*b*) Research;
(*c*) Exchange of information;
(*d*) Financial, technical and material assistance.

Recommendation 17

It is recommended that Governments and the Secretary-General take immediate steps towards the establishment of an *international fund* or a *financial institution* whose primary operative objectives will be to assist in strengthening national programmes relating to *human settlements* through the provision of seed capital and the extension of the necessary technical assistance to permit an effective mobilisation of domestic resources for housing and the environmental improvement of human settlements.

Recommendation 18

It is recommended that the following recommendations be referred to the Disaster Relief Co-ordinator for his consideration, more particularly in the context of the preparation of a report to the Economic and Social Council:

1. **It is recommended** that the Secretary-General, with the assistance of the Disaster Relief Co-ordinator and in consultation with the appropriate bodies of the United Nations system and non-governmental bodies:

(*a*) Assess the over-all requirements for the timely and widespread distribution of warnings which the observational and communications networks must satisfy:

(*b*) Assess the needs for additional observational networks and other observational systems for natural disaster detection and warnings for tropical cyclones (typhoons, hurricanes, cyclones, etc.) and their associated storm surges, torrential rains, floods, tsunamis, earthquakes, etc.;

(*c*) Evaluate the existing systems for the international communication of disaster warnings, in order to determine the extent to which these require improvement;

(*d*) On the basis of these assessments, promote, through

existing national and international organisations, the establishment of an effective world-wide natural disaster warning system, with special emphasis on tropical cyclones and earthquakes, taking full advantage of existing systems and plans, such as the World Weather Watch, the World Meteorological Organisation's Tropical Cyclone Project, the International Tsunami Warning System, the World-Wide Standardised Seismic Network and the Desert Locust Control Organisation;

(*e*) Invite the World Meteorological Organisation to promote research on the periodicity and intensity of the occurrence of droughts, with a view to developing improved forecasting techniques.

2. **It is further recommended** that the United Nations Development Programme and other appropriate international assistance agencies given priority in responding to requests from Governments for the establishment and improvement of natural disaster research programmes and warning systems.

3. **It is recommended** that the Secretary-General ensure that the United Nations system shall provide to Governments a comprehensive programme of advice and support in disaster prevention. More specifically, the question of disaster prevention should be seen as an integral part of the country programme as submitted to, and reviewed by, the United Nations Development Programme.

4. **It is recommended** that the Secretary-General take the necessary steps to ensure that the United Nations system shall assist countries with their planning for pre-disaster preparedness. To this end:

(*a*) An international programme of technical co-operation should be developed, designed to strengthen the capabilities of Governments in the field of pre-disaster planning, drawing upon the services of the resident representatives of the United Nations Development Programme;

(*b*) The Office of Disaster Relief, with the assistance of relevant agencies of the United Nations, should organise plans and programmes for international co-operation in cases of natural disasters;

(*c*) As appropriate, non-governmental international agencies and individual Governments should be invited to participate in the preparation of such plans and programmes.

GENERAL ASSEMBLY RESOLUTIONS

(a) *Institutional and financial arrangements for international environmental co-operation* – 2997 (XXVII)

The General Assembly,

Convinced of the need for prompt and effective implementation by Governments and the international community of measures designed to safeguard and enhance the human environment for the benefit of present and future generations of man,

Recognising that responsibility for action to protect and enhance the human environment rests primarily with Governments and, in the first instance, can be exercised more effectively at the national and regional levels,

Recognising further that environmental problems of broad international significance fall within the competence of the United Nations system,

Bearing in mind that international co-operative programmes in the environment field must be undertaken with due respect to the sovereign rights of States and in conformity with the Charter of the United Nations and principles of international law,

Mindful of the sectoral responsibilities of the organisations of the United Nations system,

Conscious of the significance of regional and subregional co-operation in the field of the human environment and of the important role of the regional economic commissions and other regional intergovernmental organisations,

Emphasising that problems of the human environment constitute a new and important area for international co-operation and that the complexity and interdependence of such problems require new approaches,

Recognising that the relevant international scientific and other professional communities can make an important contribution to international co-operation in the field of human environment,

Conscious of the need for processes within the United Nations system which would effectively assist developing countries to implement environmental policies and programmes that are compatible with their development plans and to participate meaningfully in international environmental programmes,

Convinced that, in order to be effective, international co-operation in the field of the human environment requires additional financial and technical resources,

Aware of the urgent need for a permanent institutional arrangement within the United Nations for the protection and improvement of the human environment,

Taking note of the report of the Secretary-General on the United Nations Conference on the Human Environment.[1]

I

Governing Council for Environmental Programmes
1. **Decides** to establish a Governing Council for Environmental Programmes composed of fifty-eight members elected by the General Assembly for three-year terms on the following basis:

(*a*) Sixteen seats for African States;
(*b*) Thirteen seats for Asian States;
(*c*) Six seats for Eastern European States;
(*d*) Ten seats for Latin American States;
(*e*) Thirteen seats for Western European and other States.

2. **Decides** that the Governing Council shall have the following main functions and responsibilities:

(*a*) To promote international co-operation in the environment field and to recommend, as appropriate, policies to this end;

(*b*) To provide general policy guidance for the direction and co-ordination of environmental programmes within the United Nations system;

(*c*) To receive and review the periodic reports of the Executive Director, referred to in section II, paragraph 1, below, on the implementation of environmental programmes within the United Nations system;

(*d*) To keep under review the world environmental situation in order to ensure that emerging environmental problems of wide international significance receive appropriate and adequate consideration by Governments;

(*e*) To promote the contribution of the relevant international scientific and other professional communities to the acquisition, assessment and exchange of environmental knowledge and information and, as appropriate, to the technical aspects of the formulation and implementation of environmental programmes within the United Nations system;

(*f*) To maintain under continuing review the impact of national and international environmental policies and measures on developing countries, as well as the problem of additional costs that may be incurred by developing countries in the implementation of environmental programmes and projects, and to ensure that such programmes and projects shall be compatible with the development plans and priorities of those countries;

(*g*) To review and approve annually the programme of utilisation of resources of the Environment Fund referred to in section III below.

3. **Decides** that the Governing Council shall report annually to the General Assembly through the Economic and Social Council, which will transmit to the Assembly such comments on the report as it may deem necessary, particularly with regard to questions of co-ordination and to the relationship of environment policies and programmes within the United Nations system to over-all economic and social policies and priorities.

II

Environment Secretariat

1. **Decides** that a small secretariat shall be established in the United Nations to serve as a focal point for environmental action and co-ordination within the United Nations system in such a way as to ensure a high degree of effective management;

2. **Decides** that the environment secretariat shall be headed by the Executive Director of the United Nations Environment Programme, who shall be elected by the General Assembly on the nomination of the Secretary-General for a term of four years and who shall be entrusted, *inter alia*, with

the following responsibilities:

(*a*) To provide substantive support to the Governing Council of the United Nations Environment Programme;

(*b*) To co-ordinate, under the guidance of the Governing Council, environmental programmes within the United Nations system, to keep their implementation under review and to assess their effectiveness;

(*c*) To advise, as appropriate and under the guidance of the Governing Council, intergovernmental bodies of the United Nations system on the formulation and implementation of environmental programmes;

(*d*) To secure the effective co-operation of, and contribution from, the relevant scientific and other professional communities from all parts of the world;

(*e*) To provide, at the request of all parties concerned, advisory services for the promotion of international co-operation in the field of the environment;

(*f*) To submit to the Governing Council, on his own initiative or upon request, proposals embodying medium-range and long-range planning for United Nations programmes in the field of the environment;

(*g*) To bring to the attention of the Governing Council any matter which he deems to require consideration by it;

(*h*) To administer, under the authority and policy guidance of the Governing Council, the Environment Fund referred to in section III below;

(*i*) To report on environmental matters to the Governing Council;

(*j*) To perform such other functions as may be entrusted to him by the Governing Council;

3. **Decides** that the costs of servicing the Governing Council and providing the small secretariat referred to in paragraph 1 above shall be borne by the regular budget of the United Nations and that operational programme costs, programme support and adminsitrative costs of the Environment Fund established under section III below shall be borne by the Fund.

III

Environment Fund

1. **Decides** that, in order to provide for additional financing for environmental programmes, a voluntary fund shall be established, with effect from 1 January 1973, in accordance with existing United Nations financial procedures;

2. **Decides** that, in order to enable the Governing Council of the United Nations Environment Programme to fulfil its activities, the Environment Fund shall finance wholly or partly the costs of the new environmental initiatives undertaken within the United Nations system — which will include the initiatives envisaged in the Action Plan for the Human Environment[2] adopted by the United Nations Conference on the Human Environment, with particular attention to integrated projects, and such other environmental activities as may be decided upon by the Governing Council — and that the Governing Council shall review these initiatives with a view to taking appropriate decisions as to their continued financing;

3. **Decides** that the Environment Fund shall be used for financing such programmes of general interest as regional and global monitoring, assessment and data-collecting systems, including, as appropriate, costs for national counterparts; the improvement of environmental quality management; environmental research; information exchange and dissemination; public education and training; assistance for national, regional and global environmental institutions; the promotion of environmental research and studies for the development of industrial and other technologies best suited to a policy of economic growth compatible with adequate environmental safeguards; and such other programmes as the Governing Council may decide upon; and that in the implementation of such programmes due account should be taken of the special needs of the developing countries;

4. **Decides** that, in order to ensure that the development priorities of developing countries shall not be adversely affected, adequate measures shall be taken to provide additional financial resources on terms compatible with the economic situation of the recipient developing country, and

that, to this end, the Executive Director, in co-operation with competent organisations, shall keep this problem under continuing review;

5. **Decides** that the Environment Fund, in pursuance of the objectives stated in paragraphs 2 and 3 above, shall be directed to the need for effective co-ordination in the implementation of international environmental programmes of the organisations of the United Nations system and other international organisations;

6. **Decides** that, in the implementation of programmes to be financed by the Environment Fund, organisations outside the United Nations system, particularly those in the countries and regions concerned, shall also be utilised as appropriate, in accordance with the procedures established by the Governing Council, and that such organisations are invited to support the United Nations environmental programmes by complementary initiatives and contributions;

7. **Decides** that the Governing Council shall formulate such general procedures as are necessary to govern the operations of the Environmental Fund.

IV

Environment Co-ordination Board

1. **Decides** that, in order to provide for the most efficient co-ordination of United Nations environmental programmes, an Environmental Co-ordinating Board, under the chairmanship of the Executive Director, should be established under the auspices and within the framework of the Administrative Committee on Co-ordination;

2. **Further decides** that the Environmental Co-ordinating Board shall meet periodically, for the purpose of ensuring co-operation and co-ordination among all bodies concerned in the implementation of environmental programmes and that it shall report annually to the Governing Council of the United Nations Environment Programme;

3. **Invites** the organisations of the United Nations system to adopt the measures that may be required to undertake

concerted and co-ordinated programmes with regard to international environmental problems, taking into account existing procedures for prior consultation, particularly on programme and budgetary matters;

4. **Invites** the regional economic commissions and the United Nations Economic and Social Office at Beirut, in co-operation where necessary with other appropriate regional bodies, to intensify further their efforts directed towards contributing to the implementation of environmental programmes in view of the particular need for the rapid development of regional co-operation in this field;

5. **Also invites** other intergovernmental and those non-governmental organisations that have an interest in the field of the environment to lend their full support and collaboration to the United Nations with a view to achieving the largest possible degree of co-operation and co-ordination;

6. **Calls upon** Governments to ensure that appropriate national institutions shall be entrusted with the task of the co-ordination of environmental action, both national and international;

7. **Decides** to review as appropriate, at its thirty-first session, the above institutional arrangements, bearing in mind, *inter alia*, the responsibilities of the Economic and Social Council under the Charter of the United Nations.

2112th plenary meeting
15 December 1972

(b) *Criteria governing multilateral financing of housing and human settlements* — 2998 (XVII)

The General Assembly,

Having considered the report of the United Nations Conference on the Human Environment,[3]

Recalling its resolutions 1393 (XIV) of 20 November 1959, 1508 (XV) of 12 December 1960, 1676 (XVI) of 18 December 1961, 1917 (XVIII) of 5 December 1963, 2036 (XX) of 7 December 1965, 2598 (XXIV) of 16 December 1969, 2626 (XXV) of 24 October 1970 and 2718 (XXV) of 15 December 1970,

Recalling also Economic and Social Council resolution 1170 (XLI) of 5 August 1966,

Mindful of the aims expressed in the preamble of the Charter of the United Nations to employ international machinery for the promotion of the economic and social advancement of all peoples, as well as in Articles 55 and 56 of the Charter,

Taking into account the *World Plan of Action for the Application of Science and Technology to Development*,[4]

Considering the important role assigned to housing as part of the International Development Strategy for the Second United Nations Development Decade,[5]

Further recalling resolution 2718 (XXV) in which the General Assembly sets out broad directions and measures essential for the improvement of human settlements,

Noting the report of the Secretary-General[6] containing proposals for action on finance for housing, building and planning,

Taking into account the annual report of the International Bank for Reconstruction and Development for 1970,[7] which, *inter alia* considered that priority should be given to housing and human settlements,

Taking note of the policy statement on urbanisation of 1972 of the International Bank for Reconstruction and Development, which, *inter alia*, reaffirms the important role of housing and human settlement in over-all national development,

Further taking note of the recognition by the International Bank for Reconstruction and Development of the need to establish appropriate national finance institutions to mobilise domestic capital to finance these activities,

Reaffirming in particular recommendations 1, 15, 16, 17 of the United Nations Conference on the Human Environment[8] adopted by the Conference,

1. that all development assistance agencies such as the United Nations Development Programme and the International Bank for Reconstruction and Development should in their development assistance activities also give high priority to requests from Governments for assistance in housing and human settlements;

2. **Recommends** that the International Bank for Reconstruction and Development in its lending policies in this sector should provide funds on terms and conditions which fully reflect the unique nature and characteristics of housing and related investments;

3. **Recommends** that in establishing criteria for eligibility for loans under more favourable terms and conditions the International Bank for Reconstruction and Development should take into account, in addition to economic and monetary criteria, such critical socio-economic factors as levels of unemployment, rates of urban growth, population density, and the general condition of the housing stock in the developing countries;

4. **Further recommends** that as a matter of priority the International Bank for Reconstruction and Development, in agreement with requesting Governments, should implement its stated policy of providing seed capital loans on favourable terms, taking into account the recommendations of paragraph 3 above, for the establishment of domestic financial institutions and organisations to mobilise and allocate capital for housing and related investments;

5. **Requests** the Secretary-General to report to the General Assembly at its twenty-eighth session on the implementation of the present resolution.

2112th plenary meeting
15 December 1972

(c) *Establishment of an international fund or financial institution for human settlements* — 2999 (XXVII)

The General Assembly,

Having considered the report of the United Nations Conference on the Human Environment,[9]

Concerned with the lack of improvement in the deplorable world housing situation, particularly the critical shortage of low-cost housing, or minimal standards of housing in developing countries,

Aware that the human environment cannot be improved in conditions of poverty, one of the palpable manifestations of which is the substandard quality of human settlements, particularly in developing countries,

Recognising the need for intensified and more concrete international action to strengthen national programmes in the planning, improvement and management of rural and urban settlements, and thereby narrowing the growing gap between housing needs and available supply and improving the environmental quality of human settlements,

Noting the report of the Secretary-General[10] on the financing of housing and community facilities,

Recalling Economic and Social Council resolutions 1170 (XLI) of 5 August 1966 and 1507 (XLVIII) 28 May 1970 on a proposed international institution to support domestic savings and credit facilities in housing;

Noting in particular recommendation 17 of the Action Plan for the Human Environment[11] adopted by the Conference that Governments and the Secretary-General should take immediate steps to establish an international fund or financial assistance for the effective mobilisation of domestic resources for housing and the environmental improvement of human settlements,

1. **Endorses** in principle the establishment of an international fund or financial institution for the purpose envisaged in recommendation 17 of the Action Plan for the Human Environment;

2. **Requests** the Secretary-General, taking into account the views expressed on this subject at the twenty-seventh session of the General Assembly, to prepare a study on the establishment and operations of such a fund or institution, together with his recommendations and proposals, and to report thereon to the Assembly at its twenty-ninth session through the Governing Council of the United Nations Environment Programme and the Economic and Social Council;

3. **Invites** the International Bank for Reconstruction and Development to collaborate in the preparation of the study indicated in paragraph 2 above.

2122th plenary meeting
15 December 1972

(d) *United Nations Conference — Exposition on Human Settlements* — 3001 (XXVII)

The General Assembly,

Recalling resolution 2718 (XXV) of 15 December 1970, in which the General Assembly recommended broad directions and measures essential for the improvement of human settlements,

Noting the urgency of the world-wide human settlement problems, present and future,

Taking into account the *World Plan of Action for the Application of Science and Technology to Development.*[12]

Considering the important role assigned to housing as part of the International Development Strategy for the Second United Nations Development Decade,[13]

Recognising the need for international efforts to develop new and additional approaches to these problems, especially in the developing countries,

Desiring to maintain the momentum of the United Nations Conference on the Human Environment in this area through a conference—exposition on human settlements, the preparation for which should generate a review of policies and programmes for human settlements, national and international, and should result in the selection and support of a series of demonstration projects on human settlements sponsored by individual countries and the United Nations,

Taking into account recommendation 2.2 of the Action Plan for the Human Environment,[14] adopted by the United Nations Conference on the Human Environment,

1. **Decides** to hold a Conference-Exposition on Human Settlements;

2. **Accepts** the offer of the Government of Canada to act as host to the Conference-Exposition in 1975;

3. **Requests** the Secretary-General to prepare and submit to the Governing Council of the United Nations Environment Programme[15] at its first session a report containing a plan for and anticipated costs of the Conference-Exposition.

2112th plenary meeting
15 December 1972

Notes

Chapter 2

1. Adna F. Weber, *The Growth of Cities in the Nineteenth Century* (New York: Macmillan, 1899; reprinted Cornell University Press, Ithaca, New York, 1963) pp. 446-51.

2. Kingsley Davis, *World Urbanisation 1950–1970*, Vol. 1 of *Basic Data for Cities, Countries and Regions* (University of California, Berkeley, Population Monograph Series No. 4, 1969).

3. United Nations, *Growth of the World's Urban and Rural Population 1920–2000* (New York: United Nations, ST/SOA/Series A/44. Sales No. E.69.XIII.3).

4. Jane Jacobs, *The Economy of Cities* (New York: Random House, 1969).

5. Edgar M. Hoover and Raymond Vernon, *Anatomy of a Metropolis* (Cambridge, Mass: Harvard University Press, 1959).

6. United Nations, *Report of the Interregional Seminar on Rural Housing and Community Facilities* (New York: United Nations, ST/TAO/Series C/103, 1968).

7. United Nations, *Rural Housing. A Review of World Conditions* (New York: United Nations, Sales No. E.69.IV.8, 1969).

8. United Nations, *Problems and Priorities in Human Settlements*, Report of the Secretary-General (New York: United Nations, A/8037, 1970).

9. E. H. Hare, 'Family Setting and the Urban Distribution of Schizophrenia', *J. Ment. Sci.* 102 (1960).

10. G. D. Klee, *An Ecological Analysis of Diagnosed Mental Illness in Baltimore*, Am. Psychiatric Assn., Report No. 22 (1967).

Chapter 3

1. United Nations Economic Commission for Africa, *Regional Physical Planning in Kenya*, a case study (United Nations, E/CN.14/HOU/35, 1969).

Israel', *United Nations Housing, Building and Planning Bulletin*, No. 12 (New York: United Nations, Sales No. 59.IV.7, 1959) p. 199.

Chapter 5

1. See *Proceedings of the First International Conference on Health Research in Housing and its Environment*, Airlie House, Virginia, 1970 (Washington, D.C.: U.S. Government Printing Office, 1970); World Health Organisation, *Expert Committee on the Public Health Aspects of Housing*, First Report (Geneva: WHO Technical Report Series, No. 225, 1961), United Nations, *Statistical Indicators of Housing Conditions* (New York: United Nations, Sales No. 62.XVIII.7, 1962); United Nations, *International Definition and Measurement of Levels of Living: An Interim Guide* (New York: United Nations, Sales No. E/CN.3/270/Rev.1. [E/CN.5/353], 1961); United Nations, *Methods for Establishing Targets and Standards for Housing and Environmental Development* (New York: United Nations, Sales No. E.68. IV.5, 1968).

2. Donald Hanson, 'Housing Policy and Programme in Tanzania', United Nations, *Interregional Advisors' Report* (New York, 1969).

3. Donald Hanson, 'Parameters for a Housing Policy in Panama', United Nations, *Interregional Advisors' Report* (New York, 1971).

4. V. Z. Newcombe, *Community Health and the Urban Environment* (Geneva: World Health Organisation, SSH/WP/ 71.3, 1971).

5. *Noise*, Report of the Committee on the Problem of Noise (London: H.M.S.O. 1963); *Quality of Dwelling and Housing Areas* Stockholm: (Swedish National Institute of Building Research, 1967).

6. United Nations, *Official Records of the Economic and Social Council, 24th Session* (New York: United Nations, E/2931,) Annex III, para. 1.

7. See United Nations, *Social Aspects and Management of Housing Projects* (New York: United Nations, E.70.IV.6,

2. Arthur Glikson, 'Rural Planning and Development in

1970) and United Nations, *Basics of Housing Management* (New York: United Nations, E.69.IV.12, 1969).

8. K. C. Rosser, 'Housing for the Lowest Income Groups: The Calcutta Experience', *Ekistics Magazine*, No. 183 (1971).

Chapter 6

1. *Man's Impact on the Global Environment: Assessment and Recommendations for Action*, Study of Critical Environmental Factors (Cambridge, Mass: The M.I.T. Press, 1970).

Chapter 7

1. Shankland, Cox and Associates, for the U.N.D.P. and the Government of S.F.R. Yugoslavia, *Master Plan for Hvar* — Proposals for the Western Half of the Island of Split (1968).

Chapter 8

1. *Disposal of Solid Toxic Wastes* (London: H.M.S.O.. 1970).

2. City of New York, Department of Traffic, *A Study of Trucking in the Garment District* (1961). See also James Decker, 'Truck Movement of Goods', in *The Urban Movement of Goods* (Organisation for Economic Co-operation and Development, 1970).

3. Vincent Ponte, 'Transportation in its Environment', *Fourth International Conference on Urban Transportation, Official Proceedings* (Pittsburg, Pa., 1969).

Chapter 9

1. United Nations, *Social Change and Social Development Policy in Latin America* (New York: United Nations, Sales No. E.70.II.9.3, 1970) p. 107.

2. Automobile Manufacturers Association, *1960 Automobile Facts and Figures* and *1970 Automobile Facts and Figures* (Detroit; 1960 and 1970).

3. Ibid.

4. Peter C. Koltnow, *Changes in Mobility in American Cities* (Washington, D.C.: Highway Users' Federation for Safety and Mobility, 1970).

5. Klaus Zimnick and the Munich Underground Railway

Board, 'Planning and Design of a Modern Public Transport System', and Hans-Jochen Vogel, 'Why Munich Needs an Underground Mass Transport System' (combined paper, mimeographed, undated).

6. P. J. Walker, 'Rapid Transit and Public Purse', *Railway Gazette International* (April 1971).

7. *Mobility Without Mayhem*, Report of the President's Task Force on Highway Safety (Washington, D.C.: U.S. Government Printing Office, 1970).

8. J. S. Robinson and R. E. Skorpie, 'The Costs of Expanding Urban Transportation – Highways Versus Rapid Transit' *Westinghouse Engineer* (Pittsburg: Westinghouse Corp., 1970).

9. Carter C. Carroll, 'Transit Progress in Europe', *Fourth International Conference on Urban Transportation* (Pittsburg, Pa., 1969).

10. See n.5 of this chapter.

11. William H Liskam, 'Transportation in its Environment – Europe', *Fourth International Conference on Urban Transportation* (Pittsburg, Pa., 1969).

Appendix
1. A/8783 and Add.1, Add.1/Corr.1 and Add.2.
2. See A/CONF.48/14 and Corr.1.
3. A/CONF.48/14 and Corr.1.
4. United Nations publication, Sales No.: E.71.II.A.18.
5. General Assembly resolution 2626 (XXV).
6. E/C.6/106.
7. International Bank for Reconstruction and Development – International Development Association, *Annual Report, 1970* (Washington, D.C.).
8. See A/CONF.48/14 and Corr.1, chap. II.
9. A/CONF.48/14 and Corr.1.
10. E/C.6/106.
11. See A/CONF.48/14 and Corr.1, chap. II.
12. United Nations publication, Sales No.: E.71.II.A.18.
13. General Assembly resolution 2626 (XXV).
14. See A/CONF.48/14 and Corr.1, chap. II.
15. See General Assembly resolution 2997 (XXVII), sect. I.